D1617002

HOUSING FINANCE IN DEVELOPING COUNTRIES

Housing Finance in Developing Countries

Robert M. Buckley
Principal Economist, Urban Division
The World Bank, Washington, DC

HD
7391
.B829
1996
West

First published in Great Britain 1996 by
MACMILLAN PRESS LTD
Houndmills, Basingstoke, Hampshire RG21 6XS
and London
Companies and representatives
throughout the world

A catalogue record for this book is available
from the British Library.

ISBN 0–333–66464–7

 First published in the United States of America 1996 by
ST. MARTIN'S PRESS, INC.,
Scholarly and Reference Division,
175 Fifth Avenue,
New York, N.Y. 10010

ISBN 0–312–16160–3

Library of Congress Cataloging-in-Publication Data
Buckley, Robert M.
Housing finance in developing countries / Robert M. Buckley.
p.   cm.
Includes bibliographical references and index.
ISBN 0–312–16160–3
1. Housing—Developing countries—Finance.
HD7391.B829   1996
338.5'82—dc20   96–26644
                                                          CIP

© Robert M. Buckley 1996

All rights reserved. No reproduction, copy or transmission of
this publication may be made without written permission.

No paragraph of this publication may be reproduced, copied or
transmitted save with written permission or in accordance with
the provisions of the Copyright, Designs and Patents Act 1988,
or under the terms of any licence permitting limited copying
issued by the Copyright Licensing Agency, 90 Tottenham Court
Road, London W1P 9HE.

Any person who does any unauthorised act in relation to this
publication may be liable to criminal prosecution and civil
claims for damages.

10   9   8   7   6   5   4   3   2   1
05   04   03   02   01   00   99   98   97   96

Printed in Great Britain by
Ipswich Book Co. Ltd, Ipswich, Suffolk

Contents

List of Figures and Tables

Figures

Tables

Preface

The work described in this book began in 1985 when Ray Struyk of the Urban Institute asked me to accompany him to India to examine the operations of the Housing Development Finance Company (HDFC) of India. It is almost quaint to recall now the perspectives on housing finance at that time. The implications of the US Savings and Loan crisis were essentially unknown. HDFC had not yet become the powerful player that it is today in the Indian financial markets. The prospects of real estate finance being a concern in cities like Moscow were implausible.

A great deal has changed in the past decade. As a World Bank economist, I've been lucky enough to have a front row seat for observing and attempting to analyze these changes. I've travelled to more than 25 countries and watched housing finance policy transform. It went from being something of a policy carbuncle, a mere conduit to carry out government policies, into an issue of major concern. It became the biggest contingent liability ever realized by the US government, as well as an engine of growth and financial stability in a number of developing countries.

In such a far-flung exercise over such a long time period I've incurred more than the usual number of debts. Bertrand Renaud, Per Ljung, Mike Cohen and Patricia Annez at the World Bank have at various times all been very supportive managers as well as good colleagues. Peter Kimm and David Olinger of USAID, and Sonia Hammam, first at USAID and later at the Bank, always were helpful in getting sometimes complicated stories straight.

This book brings together, updates, and shows the relationships between a series of papers that I wrote, often with others. My co-authors taught me a great deal. Zsuzsa Daniel, Patric Hendershott, Steve Mayo, Margret Thalwitz, and Kevin Villani were particularly enjoyable to work with, and in Kevin's case, to argue with, as were Anapam Doekeniya, Dagney Faulk, Leke Olajide, Barbara Lippman, and Thakor Persaud. I also appreciate the opportunity to republish articles that were published earlier in journals. A complete list of acknowledgements to the publishers is provided below. Of course the usual disclaimer with respect to the views not being those of the World Bank applies.

I've also had many colleagues who patiently explained how housing markets, housing finance, and financial markets work in their countries. In India, the HDFC mafia not only taught me a great deal but became some of the people I admire most. From Deepak Parekh, Nasser Munjee, Deepak Satwalekar, Pradip Shah, Kshirsagarji, and K.C. Sivaramakrishnan I learned much more than finance. In Hungary, Jozsef Hegedus, Ivan Tosics, and the late Gyula Partos were all incredible colleagues. Similarly, in Russia Eugene Gurenko, Natasha Kalinina, David Hodjaev, Anwar Shamusafarov, as well as Bertrand Renaud once again, tried to explain the chaos we were observing. In Ghana, Mrs Ansah was amazing, as were Yilmaz Arguden and Bulent Gultekin in Turkey, in getting reforms implemented.

Conversations with people like Akim Mabogunje of Nigeria, Ian Brzski of Poland, the late Laughlin Currie in Colombia, Solly Angel, and particularly Alain Bertaud, as well as a list of Indians, Bank staff, and consultants too long to begin, were great fun. They all have a way of making normal, mostly dull analytical work seem fascinating and productive. Kyung-Hwan Kim of Habitat read the entire manuscript and made many helpful comments.

Finally, the opportunity to observe and participate in this process of change has meant that I've been away far too much. My boys, Chris and Tom, have always been great about this, and I think they've caught the travel bug too from accompanying me on a number of trips. Nevertheless, even though they have helped prepare the index, they'll have to wait to have a book dedicated to them. This book is dedicated to Mary, my wife, who bore the burden of my travels and kept things going. Her patience, efficiency, love, and understanding seem to allow her to dance through all difficulties. I cannot thank her enough.

ROBERT M. BUCKLEY

Acknowledgements

An earlier version of Chapter 2 appeared as 'Housing Finance in Developing Countries; The Role of Credible Contracts', in *Economic Development and Cultural Change*, January 1994. Chapter 3 is a substantial rewrite of a paper co-authored with Stephen Mayo, 'Housing Policy in Developing Countries: Evaluating the Macroeconomic Impact', in *Review of Urban and Regional Development*, July 1989. Chapter 4 updates 'Rapid Housing Privatization in Reforming Economies: Pay the Special Dividend Now,' *Journal of Real Estate Finance and Economics*, January 1995. It was co-authored by Patric Hendershott and Kevin Villani. A UK-oriented version of Chapter 5 was published in *Urban Studies* as 'A Simple Theory of the UK Housing Sector', vol. 2, 1982. The first chapter of section 2, that is, Chapter 6, was published as 'Mortgage Design under Inflation and Real Wage Uncertainty: The Use of a Dual Indexed Mortgage', in *World Development* in vol. 3, 1993. It was written with Barbara Lippman and Thakor Persaud. Zsuzsa Daniel and Margret Thalwitz were co-authors of Chapter 8, which was published in Hungarian in *Kozgazdasagi Szemle*, in 1995. Chapter 9 appeared as 'The Measurement, Targeting, and Control of Housing Finance Subsidies', in *Public Finance/Finances Publiques*, vol. 3, 1991. An earlier version of the Chapter 10 appeared in the *Journal of African Studies* as 'Private Sector Participation, Structural Adjustment and Nigeria's New National Housing Policy: Lessons from Foreign Experience'. It was written with Dagney Faulk and Leke Olajide. Finally, earlier versions of Chapters 7 and 11 appeared as World Bank working papers. Anupam Dokeniya co-authored the former.

1 Introduction

In the past 15 years perspectives on the functioning of markets in general, and the financial markets in particular have undergone unprecedented change. This has been a period of the greatest volatility in inflation and interest rates in history. Not coincidentally it has been a time of international debt crisis.[1] It has also been a time when the fall of communism has led to the bankruptcy of dirigiste schemes that ignore the efficiency aspects of government policy. Market processes are now universally recognized as the most effective way to allocate resources. In the wake of these changes have come enormous adjustments in both financial markets and public policy.

Financial intermediation is now on a global scale. It relies on a wide range of new financial products, such as securitization and synthetic assets, to allocate the various risks and services provided by financial instruments. The public policy arena has also changed. It now gives much greater attention to the sustainability, transparency, and even the contingencies implied by the instruments of public policy. For example, in the past five years alone, more than 20 countries have adopted two of the most fundamental features of sustainable, transparent governance – that is, two-tiered banking systems and national income taxes.

It is difficult to exaggerate the implications that these changes have for the way housing is financed and provided throughout the world. In a word, housing finance systems and traditional public housing delivery mechanisms, have become obsolete. True, the old systems have been creaking along for a number of years, but two aspects of the changed world environment will put these systems to rest in the coming years.

First, housing's traditional funding source is disappearing. In developed and many developing economies, housing has typically been financed through term and denomination intermediation within the household sector. That is, families borrowed relatively small, long-term mortgage loans financed with even smaller short-term deposits, also provided by the household sector.[2] It has been exactly these components of the financial system – term risks and denomination transformation – that have experienced the most significant increases in competition. In developed economies, mortgages are no longer small loans issued by local, often mutually-based investor funds. Through securitization and mortgage bonds, mortgages have become attractive investments to long-term portfolio investors, such as pension funds and insurance companies. Indeed, by 1992 the volume of outstanding mortgage securities in the US exceeded the capitalization of the American Stock Exchange.[3] Similarly, in Europe, building societies are becoming banks, and specialized housing-finance circuits are disappearing. Local household-oriented, savings institutions are losing the competition for previously protected, localized deposit markets.[4]

In most developing and reforming economies, the changes are even more fundamental. In many of these countries, and particularly reforming socialist and Latin American economies, it is not just a contraction of an industry that has occurred, but the *de facto* elimination of one. Few of the traditional household 'banks' have been able to remain viable through the shocks of inflation or economic reform. In many other developing countries, in which there was effectively no housing finance system, such as India, brand new housing finance systems are beginning to emerge.

Second, the old systems have become too expensive, often in unanticipated ways. For example, the losses from the distress of existing housing finance system in the US resulted in hundreds of billions of dollars of government expenditures. But the US case was by no means an isolated incident. Problems in housing-finance systems in the UK, Germany, Sweden, and Finland, resulted in 'negative equity' for large numbers of families, or largely unanticipated government obligations for the sector. Similar problems arose in such different economies as Hungary, Argentina, and Zimbabwe. As a result of these costs, more effort is being placed on developing broader measures of the effects of policy. It has become clearer that although budgeted expenditures for housing typically account for a small share of government expenditures, about 2 to 3 percent, these measures tell little about the resource costs of various housing and housing-finance policies.[5] The heightened interest in the transparency and efficiency of policy requires greater attention be given to what the government does 'off the books' to the price of such a large portion of wealth.

This book examines the way these changes have affected the financing and delivery of housing in developing and reforming economies. It is divided into two parts: a framework for analysis in Chapters 2 to 5, and applications of the framework in case studies in Chapters 6 through 11. A main emphasis throughout is the demonstration of the gains that can be realized from overcoming the often blurred distinctions between fiscal and financial policies for housing. A final chapter traces through the evolution of World Bank-supported projects in the sector. It also provides a summary of some of the principles of effective housing-finance systems.

Part I: The Framework for Analysis

The first three chapters of Part I each deals with a policy 'handle' through which the sector can be affected, that is, the financial, real sector, and fiscal aspects of policy. Chapter 5 brings these perspectives together in a simple model of the housing sector. The model is similar in spirit to the models used in intermediate macroeconomics. While a model of this sort can help show the interactions between the various perspectives, it is by no means a unifying, or for that matter essential, part of the analysis. Rather, it is something of an analytical benchmark. It helps show the linkages among the perspectives discussed in the preceding chapters. It also helps clarify the assumptions or empirical evidence needed to evaluate the likely effects of a specific policy. Under what circumstances, for example, would one expect a credit program to affect the quantity of housing produced or the price of housing?

The emphasis in Chapter 2 is on the financial aspects of housing-finance policy. It discusses the important role that credible financial contracts can play in the development of housing finance. The chapter suggests that in most developing countries it is the lack of postcontract governance rather than the cost of producing contracts that explains the restrained supply of mortgage credit. Some examples of ways to develop credible contracts are drawn from India, and data from a number of developing countries are presented. In terms of the conceptual linkages to the other policy areas, the financial-sector issues can be seen as being comparable to the LM curve of IS-LM-like analysis of Chapter 5.

In Chapter 3, the emphasis is on identifying and measuring-off budget components of fiscal policy with respect to housing and housing finance. Some of the motivations for the pursuit of such policies' – such as financial repression, central planners' choices, and even the unintended consequences of broader policy actions – are discussed. The chapter reports regression results on housing investment as a share of gross domestic product (GDP) from a 50-country sample, and shows how this pattern behaved before and during the debt crisis. Then, it discusses some examples of the types of implicit policies that have been pursued. Particular emphasis is given to identifying the links between these policies and trends in housing investment. Finally, the Polish case is briefly reviewed. It provides a particularly striking example of the misleading sense of policy that can be inferred from a traditional public-finance perspective. In terms of integrating the policy perspectives in Chapter 5, this chapter can be seen as similar in notion to the aggregate expenditure concerns of an IS curve.

Chapter 4 focuses on real sector policies. In particular, it focuses on the privatization of publicly-owned housing in reforming socialist economies. It critically reviews the arguments that have been made against privatizing the housing stock. It also discusses the problems implied by a failure to address housing-sector distortions before housing finance is integrated into financial markets. From Chapter 5's perspective, the real sector issues can be considered by analogy to the labor market. These issues focus on how rigidities in the housing market can cause shifts in demand to be accommodated by changes in quantities or prices.

Chapter 5 develops a simple model for examining the interaction of financial, fiscal, and real sector policies. At its simplest level, this chapter provides a schema for considering how an increase in the rate of inflation might affect the demand for housing and the supply of mortgage credit. But, more interestingly, it also shows how these two effects interact. On the one hand, the chapter could be skipped without disrupting the analysis; on the other hand, it brings the various perspectives together in a simple framework that will be familiar to those with undergraduate training in macroeconomics. Hence, the chapter should help integrate the various dimensions of policy analysis.

Part II: Case Studies

Two of the five case studies focus on financial aspects of housing finance, and three deal with the fiscal/real sector issues. Chapter 11 closes Part II with a broad review of World Bank experience with housing finance projects.

Chapter 6 reviews the problems that have been experienced in designing mortgage instruments in an inflationary environment. Approaches that addressed either the concerns of lenders (through indexation to inflation) or those of some borrowers provided disincentives to lenders. In principle, in many circumstances systems can be developed which safeguard the interests of both groups while providing for continued lending. However, given the need for caution on controlling implicit subsidies considerable care must be taken, particularly when inflation exceeds 30 percent per year. This chapter presents some simulations of the risks and contingent liabilities of various instruments in different economic environments.

Chapter 7 considers the role of mortgage finance in Colombia's economic growth. It first traces out the relationship of mortgage finance to the supply of monetary balances. Then, it builds on empirical work that demostrated the significance of monetary balances for growth by estimating an aggregate production function. The equation is estimated for Colombia in the 1980s. It shows that mortgage innovations played a significant role in explaining the country's growth and financial resilience.

The Colombian case is interesting because – following the recommendations of Lauchlin Currie, the director of the first World Bank mission to Colombia and President Roosevelt's chief economic advisor – indexed mortgages were introduced in 1972 and played a major role in the development of Colombia's deposit markets. It is also interesting because of all the Latin American economies, the competitive Colombian financial system most effectively weathered the debt crisis of the 1980s. The Colombian mortgage reforms did not simply deregulate the interest rate on deposits and thereby permit a more competitive market for broadly-defined monetary balances. Colombia induced more competition. Indexed mortgages permitted mortgage lenders to pay higher yields on deposits than those available at commercial banks. As a result, other depository institutions had to compete for deposits.

Chapter 8 contrasts with Chapter 7's discussion of policy success. It examines the destabilizing effects that bad housing-finance policy can have. It considers the kinds of housing subsidies that are channeled through housing-finance systems in economies experiencing high inflation and financial stress. The chapter shows the destabilizing effects Argentina's housing-subsidy system had on the country's stabilization policy in the late 1980s, presenting measures of the implicit transfers and welfare costs of housing policy. It shows that both the subsidies and the welfare costs were very large, as high as 5 to 6 percent of GDP. Policies that would improve the targeting and transparency of the subsidies and reduce the welfare losses are also discussed.

In Chapter 9 the evolution and economic costs of socialist housing policy are examined. While the emphasis in this chapter is on the Hungarian experience, the questions considered also apply to other reforming countries. For instance, how can the paradox of a very costly housing-subsidy system be reconciled with the housing shortages that characterize all the reforming economies? And, how did the housing policies of reformed socialist systems compare with those of market economies? It also identifies the kinds of empirical data needed to draw firm inferences about policy in post-reform systems. Finally, it provides some illustrative calculations of the welfare costs of such systems for China, Poland, Russia, and Hungary.

Chapter 10 focuses on the housing finance policy introduced in Nigeria in 1992. It considers the program in light of Nigeria's ongoing, structural adjustment program, and its housing market structure. The language of the new policy approach embraces the private sector as the chief means to address the severe shortages of shelter. It also calls for the 'government to become an enabler, promoter and facilitator conducive to individual and co-operative housing efforts'. This is in contrast to the traditional perspective of government as a direct implementer of housing policy. However, the financial instruments proposed will not fulfill these objectives. Indeed, they may well have the opposite effect: increasing the role of the public sector and expanding the distortions that have undermined the functioning of the housing market. Chapter 10 also reviews strategies and programs that other countries have used under similar circumstances to restructure their shelter sector.

Chapter 11 reviews the World Bank's experience with housing-finance loans. It categorizes the various Bank-supported housing finance projects according to the book's three policy dimensions – that is, financial, fiscal and real sector distortions. It also discusses the general performance of the projects and their evolution.

Chapter 12, the conclusion, presents a perspective on how Bank work in this area has changed to emphasize financial intermediation. Housing-finance reforms are discussed in light of the risks and rewards of innovations in these systems. Perhaps the overarching theme of the conclusion is that the institutions involved in housing-finance systems are often complex, highly idiosyncratic, and developed almost through the accumulation of the accidents of history. Consequently, there is no single way to implement efficiency-enhancing housing finance reforms. Nevertheless, even though the approaches to reform can vary a great deal, the basic principles of effective housing finance are straightforward and worth identifying, Indeed, it is only through clarity about these principles that the distortions and risks of the existing systems can be effectively addressed.

Part I

The Framework for Analysis

2 The Financial Policy Dimension

2.1 INTRODUCTION

In most developing countries, relatively little mortgage credit is voluntarily supplied. The main reason for this is the lack of credible contracts of the sort dicussed by Oliver Williamson (1985). The cost of postcontract governance rather than the cost of producing contracts explains this restrained supply of mortgage credit. This is an important distinction because the costs of production are dictated by technological conditions – that is, the nature of the production function – and consequently little can be done to change them. The costs of governance, however, are more amenable to change. Hence, if there are significant gains from reducing these costs, institutional reforms may help realize them.

This chapter examines the qualities of housing investment that affect the costs of contract governance. The second topic of this chapter is a discussion of the gains implied by improved governance of mortgage contracts. The chief gain is that housing finance systems in most developing countries would be able to grow spontaneously and rapidly. This growth, in turn, would improve shelter conditions as well as the efficiency of financial systems.

The plan of the chapter is as follows. Sections 2.2 and 2.3 briefly discuss why relatively little mortgage credit is supplied by formal financial intermediaries in developing countries. Sections 2.4 and 2.5 consider the particular qualities of housing investments that Section 2.3 suggests have a bearing on the demand for and supply of housing finance. The qualities are housing's durability and its potential strength as collateral. Section 2.6 compares the role of governance and production costs by explaining the kinds of housing finance systems that are observed in developing countries such as India.

2.2   HOUSING, HOUSING FINANCE AND THE ECONOMY

Housing investment typically amounts to 3–8 percent of gross domestic product (GDP) and 15 to 30 percent of gross fixed capital formation. It is usually the largest single form of household wealth and accounts for between one-quarter and one-half of the capital stock in developed and developing countries.[1] However, the share of housing investment financed through formal financial intermediaries is very small in almost all developing countries, and housing finance accounts for only a small share of financial assets.

Table 2.1 presents estimates of the ratio of net new mortgage lending from the formal financial sector to the level of housing investment for a number of economies. It indicates that in developing countries a much greater share of housing investment comes from internally generated funds. The average ratio of mortgage credit supplied by the formal sector was less than 22 percent of housing investment in developing countries, or about one-fourth the level of the Organization for Economic Cooperation and Development (OECD) countries. (If Colombia, with its very effective housing finance system (see Chapter 7) is excluded as atypical of developing countries, the average falls to 16 percent.) In all of the countries surveyed, home mortgages account for an insignificant share of financial assets. This indicates a shift from the beginning of the century, when home mortgages accounted for more than 20 percent of financial assets in the countries examined by Raymond Goldsmith.[2]

Credible Contracts and Housing Finance

When properly constructed, housing is the most durable fixed capital in the economy, and its value is one of the most impervious to use.[3] Furthermore, because people need housing throughout their lifetime, and a house often forms part of families' bequests to their heirs, it accounts for a large part of household wealth. Of course, producing housing with materials with a short lifetime, as is often done in developing countries, can reduce housing's durability.

Housing's durability affects the demand for its financing. When the long asset life of the investment is combined with its lumpy, largely nonpecuniary services the result is that housing production often needs financing in order to be undertaken. For such financing

Table 2.1 Increase in housing credit (HC) as a share of housing investment (HI), selected countries

Country	HC/HI
Mexico	.02
India	.10
Turkey	.08
Malaysia	.50
Morocco	.15
Colombia	.75
United Kingdom	.58
Kenya	.11
Tunisia	.11
Korea	.20
Pakistan	.11
Philippines	.26
Portugal	.20
Senegal	.06
Thailand	.33
United States	1.26
Canada	.76
OECD average excluding the United States and Turkey	.85

Source: See Buckley (1994) for original sources. The time period is the early 1980s.

to be most effective it should have a maturity similar to the asset life or the expected length of the resident's working life; that is, financing should be long-term. This kind of long-term contract requires a set of rules for determining how the contractual obligations might be modified if the circumstances of the borrower or lender change during the contract.

Housing is a form of wealth that, in principle, can be transferred with less loss of value than is the case for most other assets. It is, in short, a highly redeployable asset. Consequently, the contractual rules governing its long-term financing can be relatively straightforward from a strictly financial perspective. If the loan is not repaid, the house can be reclaimed with lower relative loss. In contrast, a loan to an investor in a steel plant, for example, will incur a loss if the venture fails. The plant is highly specialized and can only produce steel; the house can be redeployed to provide services to

the employees of other industries. It can be sold or rented to workers of a more successful venture. More important, the steel-plant
employees' skills are also more flexible than is the plant's capital.
These employees can change jobs and continue to repay their loans.
Households will not always have such options. Often, however, they
are likely to have more options than specialized investors. As a
result, the type of contract written should be simpler or the price of
inducing a lender to bear this risk should be lower.

Unfortunately, from a social perspective, contract resolution in
the event of a change in the ability to repay is anything but straightforward. Eviction is a difficult procedure even when it is seen as a
fair and reasonable reaction to the behavior of a borrower. For
example, the eviction of a poor family that has had bad luck (such
as the loss of income caused by the death of the wage earner)
can easily prompt sympathetic protections of the borrower. Unfortunately, when these protections become all-encompassing, it becomes difficult to supply credible contracts that protect lenders from
risks that could be exploited if circumstances permit. In such environments, housing finance's inherent safety due to housing's
redeployability is more than offset by the lenders' having little recourse to remedies.

A second characteristic affecting housing's collateral strength is
its real-denominated return. In urbanizing economies with limited
savings options, housing can be one of the principal savings vehi-
cles. Bacause its return is in real (rather than nominal) terms it is
less affected by changes in financial regulations, such as interest-
rate ceilings, than are other investments. Neither do investments in
housing appear to be as adversely affected by unanticipated increases
in the inflation rate as returns to many other investments (see Gultekin,
1983). Finally, both theory and empirical evidence suggest that housing's value is likely to increase as economies urbanize, regardless
of the efficacy of the financial system. Ultimately, the price and
attractiveness of real-denominated assets, such as housing, depend
fundamentally on the credibility and breadth of the financial system. When financial policies cause financial assets to yield negative
real returns, households opportunistically avoid these 'taxes on saving' by saving in the form of bricks and mortar. Therefore, because
of the nature of its return, housing affords a means of avoiding
many of government's attempts to tax or allocate household sav-

ings. The more uncertain the policy environment, the better the collateral it affords.

2.3 HOUSING'S DURABILITY AND CREDIT AFFORDABILITY

Housing's durability has very basic effects on the affordability of both housing and the debt that is needed to finance it. Because a house is long-lived and its rental cost reqires a significant share of annual income, the present value of housing is a multiple of annual income. As a result, ownership of housing can easily be beyond the reach of many families and there is little that fiscal or financial policy can do to relieve this problem. In contrast, the mortgage debt affordability problem can often be greatly reduced by changes in the housing finance policy.

The Mortgage Repayment Tilt Problem

Mortgage debt affordability is an insidious problem because, unlike most other sectors of the economy, changes in the inflation rate can make it less affordable. As a result, housing can become less affordable without any change in real income or real prices. Inflation can have such 'real-side' effects on the efficacy of mortgage contracts because of the nature of long-term mortgage debt contracts written in nominal terms. Even low rates of inflation redistribute real mortgage repayments toward the early years of a mortgage loan, making payments out of income in those years more difficult (see Lessard and Modigliani, 1975). As is discussed in detail in Chapter 6, this change in borrowing costs is a redistribution of real costs, not an increase in costs. Unfortunately, this redistribution is in a direction that is opposite to the one preferred by families whose income can keep pace with inflation over the longer term.

The Policy Response to Mortgage Affordability Problems

Policy-makers in developing countries have responded to mortgage affordability problems in two basic ways: through credit subsidies and through redesign of the mortgage contract. The problems with the credit subsidies' approach are well known (see Renaud, 1984). This section, therefore, considers the redesign of the mortgage contract. This approach usually involves some form of indexation of repayments, which attempts to immunize the real value of mortgage repayments from the high and uncertain rate of inflation anticipated at loan origination.

In high-inflation countries, such as those of Latin America, mortgage indexation was introduced to ameliorate housing affordability problems. Although a number of observers, for example Milton Friedman (1974a), have suggested that these instruments were introduced to facilitate the contracting undertaken by two parties in an inflationary environment, this has not in fact, been the case. The movement away from the use of nominal-interest rate, level-payment mortgage schedules (as occurred in Chile in 1959, Brazil in 1964, Colombia in 1972, Argentina in 1976, Mexico in 1988, Turkey in 1989, Ghana and Poland in 1992, and Hungary in 1994) was the result of government policies dictating that housing banks and government funds offer such loans. It was not the result of market participants freely modifying their contracting methods. While indexed contracts were a cost-effective means of restructuring mortgages to redistribute the high real initial costs of borrowing, and reduce government transfers, they were not an effective means of introducing the kinds of credible contracts that would induce investors to share the risks posed by indexation. In cases without active private sector involvement, over the longer term problems arose.

The main problem has been that loan repayments were often indexed to wages rather than to prices, and steady real-wage growth stopped. When real-wage reductions occurred, the indexes produced automatic loan forgiveness rather than loan forbearance. Forgiveness applied equally to those whose wages outperformed the general index and those whose wages did not. In this respect, the indexes were a form of real-wage insurance rather than a mortgage contract. An indexed loan increases the lenders' exposure to real economic risks. However, the use of indexes that automatically discount the borrower's liability if average real wages do not increase does more than increase the riskiness of such loans. If the real interest charged does not compensate for these additional risks, the loan terms create a situation in which the contract is not credible. In such an environment only publicly supported and implicitly subsidized lenders will participate.

For mortgage affordability concerns (rather than housing affordability problems), price indexation has much to recommend it, particularly relative to credit subsidies. With indexed repayments, long-term mortgages can be attractive investments for long-term investors. However, it is difficult to exaggerate the importance of the credibility of mortgage design to the success of such efforts. Equally important is the need to recognize the likelihood that such instruments will not perform in financial environments in which inflation remains at extremely high and volatile levels. Hence, the costs and benefits of mortgage indexation depend on the design of the instrument and the economic environment. Ultimately, however, because of housing's durability in inflationary environments, mortgage design must take real – as opposed to nominal – repayments into account. Otherwise, the cash-flow problems of mortgage contracting, rather than rates of return on investment, will dominate decision-making with respect to housing investment.

2.4 HOUSING'S COLLATERAL EFFICIENCY

Housing can be a relatively strong form of collateral because of its asset qualities, particularly its redeployability,. Two types of evidence are adduced to support this view: (1) the relative volatility of house prices in a number of countries, and (2) the relative price paid to bear this risk in a well-functioning credit market.

Lower relative-price volatility is an important determinant of the value of an asset's collateral value. It is important because relative constancy makes it less likely that the value of the asset financed will fall below the value of the debt used to finance it. Table 2.2 presents data on the volatility of house prices compared to that of an investment in equities in a number of countries. Housing's relatively low volatility implies that the risk of households repaying mortgage loans should be lower than the risks associated with financing more price-volatile assets. The table presents the coefficient of variation of time-series data on the real price of housing and the stock market indexes for various types of economies: developing countries with high inflation rates that have experienced substantial real shocks, a relatively low-inflation developing economy, a high-growth-rate developing country, and developed low- and high-inflation economies. With real interest rate and income changes, real house prices fell in all cases, sometimes sharply. However, in no case was the drop anything like the reduction in stock market values. Italy experienced the highest relative real house-price volatility, and this was less than half the volatility of the stock market index. Of course, relative asset and liability value alone do not determine whether default occurs. For example, even if the outstanding debt does exceed the value of the property, households often do not default because of the indirect costs to them of doing so – the loss in the value of their reputation, and so on.[4]

Because most home-owners own only one house, the cross-sectional variance of the return to housing and its covariance with the returns on other assets is also very important in evaluating housing's collateral efficiency. Sufficient data do not exist with respect to housing's cross-sectional variance. However, Benjamin Friedman (1985) has examined housing's covariance properties. He concludes that in the United States housing investments are much less risky than investments in debt, either short- or long-term, or equities. He shows that even if the return to housing has a high cross-sectional variance, a fall in house prices is likely to be contemporaneous with a smaller decline in total wealth than is the case for a fall in the value of other forms of wealth. As a result, housing investments will tend to be safe relative not only to specific investments but also to investments that are diversified across economies. This collateral strength of housing implies that market-rate credit for this asset should carry a lower interest rate, all other things held constant, than the interest rate charged to a borrower with less secure asset collateral.

A lower interest rate for mortgages is exactly what is observed in markets where the price of this kind of risk can be inferred. For instance, the interest rate increase needed to compensate for the risk associated with possible default on mortgages in the United States has, according to Cunningham and Hendershott (1984), been in the order of 0.5 percent per annum for loans with loan-to-value ratios of 90 percent. This credit-risk fee is about one-seventh of the risk fee charged many US corporate borrowers at about the same point in time.[5]

Table 2.2 Coefficients of variation of house prices and stock market
indexes

Country	House prices	Stock index	Index/house prices
Argentina	.090	.399	4.3
Brazil	.060	.325	5.4
Italy	.114	.294	2.6
Korea	.081	.471	5.8
Malaysia	.027	.120	4.4
United Kingdom	.075	.20	2.7
United States	.063	.141	2.2
Average	.073	.279	3.8

Source: Buckley (1994).

Borrowers' Concerns with Housing's Collateral Efficiency

Borrowers' concerns with housing's collateral efficiency arise because
of the long-run fungibility of credit. That is, over the long run,
households attempt to finance their investments with the lowest cost
credit. As has been stressed, if housing provides the safest collateral, all other things being constant, it should also be one of the
least costly ways to borrow. This view was first made with respect
to mortgage credit by Meltzer (1974). He showed that over the
twentieth century the share of mortgage credit in household liabilities in the United States grew much more rapidly than did the share
of housing in household wealth. This pattern suggests that households use the increased mortgage indebtedness to finance assets other
than housing. In other words, households rely on mortgages as a
means to borrow because it is the cheapest way to issue debt and
not because of what the debt explicitly finances.

For borrowers in developing countries, restrictions on being able
to rely on the collateral efficiency of housing are likely to be more
important than in developed countries. This occurs because, as discussed by Hayashi *et al.* (1988), in developing countries there are
fewer other ways to collateralize the human capital that accounts
for most of household wealth. As a result, the cost implied by restricting access to market-rate mortgage credit is higher in these
countries. If one takes a life-cycle view of consumer behavior, clearly

it is younger households that bear most of the incidence of this restriction.

Lender Concerns with Housing's Collateral Efficiency

In developing countries lender concerns with housing's collateral efficiency arise for two reasons. First, the technical insolvency of such a large portion of development finance institutions in developing countries indicates that *ex post* these lenders have assumed underpriced risks.[6] An important part of any restructuring strategy for these institutions should be encouragement of safer lending. Housing's collateral efficiency suggests that correctly priced mortgage finance can be part of this 'flight to safety'. The need for less risky lending is particularly true of financial systems that are deregulating and removing portfolio restrictions. Less constrained lenders are by definition able to take more risks, and investing in market-rate mortgages can be part of a risk-tempering deregulation strategy.[7]

Second, as shown in Chapter 3, financiers of few other assets can reasonably assume that demand for assets they are financing will be income-elastic over a wide range of development. Mortgage intermediation can be expected to yield not only a safe positive return to savers, it will also provide a growing source of relatively safe income with which to mobilize the financial savings of the household sector. By providing market-rate mortgage credit, as well as the traditional deposit-taking services, intermediaries may be able to more effectively mobilize more financial resources from households. The result can be an expanding, more buoyant, and competitive financial system. Therefore, rather than being viewed as yet another claimant on an inelastic supply of financial resources, housing finance can afford a way to reduce financial market segmentation and narrowness.

The Policy Response to Housing's Collateral Efficiency

In few developing countries are lenders able to exploit the inherent collateral safety of housing loans. When land tenure rights are ambiguous, or foreclose proceedings uncertain, what in principle is a low-risk loan, becomes a high-risk one in practice. For example, an Indian government study, the Shah Report (1978), showed that is could take 'not less than ten years' to foreclose on a mortgage borrower who had not made payments.

Such a basis for proceeding is both inefficient and an encouragement to act in financially disreputable ways. Similarly, while public investment in land titling and recording systems may be a significant expenditure, lack of such titles forces borrowers to rely on their next most effective forms of collateral, which for many borrowers are either nonexistent or much more expensive (for example, pawn shops). In India, since 1978, a privately owned, joint stock company, the Housing Development Finance Company of Bombay (HDFC), has used an effective way to circumvent these kinds of contract enforcement problems.

2.5 CREDIBLE CONTRACTS AND THE GROWTH OF HOUSING-FINANCE SYSTEMS

According to Morris (1985), as of 1980 formal housing finance in India was virtually nonexistent, even though the rest of the financial system was highly developed. The explanation offered for this state of affairs correspond to what might be termed a traditional economic explanation. That is, the systems have not existed because at market prices they have not been wanted. According to this view, the systems are not wanted because the *ex ante* administrative costs of the loans are too high, the size of an affordable loan is too low to interest investors, and formal lenders cannot compete with the loan terms made available through the inter-family or informal loan market. The result, then, is little or no supply of formal housing finance because at the market price there has been little or no demand. According to this view, the technological constraints are prohibitive.

Reconsidering the High *Ex Ante* Cost Explanation

The high *ex ante* cost explanation has two premises: (1) when administrative costs per mortgage loan are combined with small loan sizes, the effective borrowing costs are sufficiently high that demand for credit is discouraged; and (2) even if the first point is inaccurate, the proportion of income that households are able to pay to service mortgage debt payments is such that the aggregate demand for this credit is not likely to be a major credit market activity. For India, both of these premises are dubious, as the growth in the Indian housing finance system over the 1990s has made clear.

The high administrative cost argument is, of course, correct in an absolute sense. There are some fixed costs that are relatively invariant with respect to loan size; call these costs F. These are the administrative costs of getting a clear title and checking the applicant's income figures. Amortizing these costs over smaller loan sizes necessarily results in higher effective interest rates, $F + R$, where R is the risk-free cost of funds. These higher rates, in turn, will reduce the demand for mortgage credit. However, the amount by which these higher administrative costs increase the total cost of borrowing, C, is almost certainly less than the amount by which housing's collateral safety could reduce the risk premium, D, which lenders require. In other words, $C = R + F + D$, and the increase in F associated with the small size of a mortgage may be more than offset by the reduction in D. For example, mortgage loans made by private mortgage lenders in India earn a spread of less than 3 percent over the cost of funds that have the same maturity as the mortgages. This spread compensates for both F and D, and it is less than half the increase in borrowing costs that Timberg and Aiyar (1984) found for unsecured loans relative to secured loans in India. When both of these costs are taken into account, mortgages are an inexpensive way to borrow. Hence, the appropriate benchmark for considering how administrative costs are likely to affect demand, is their effect relative to the cost differential on secured and unsecured loans.

The second *ex ante* line of argument as to why there is little or no demand for housing finance in developing countries – that household repayment capacity limits demand – is flawed for two reasons. First, it focuses only on flows of income and minimum housing costs rather than on possible adjustments of houshold portfolios. Second, it understates demand by relying on expenditures on housing consumption as a measure of how much people would be willing to pay for homes.

An example of the first type of argument is made as a general argument by Grimes (1976) and as a particular argument for India by Mohan (1987). The latter estimates that if households in India were willing to spend 20 to 30 percent of their income on mortgage repayments, and the credit markets would accommodate these demands, the aggregate share of mortgages in credit market activity would not reach significant levels. The lack of activity would occur because few households could afford the minimum housing unit.

This line of argument overlooks the fact that in 1978 household holdings of gold and precious metals in India were equal to 70 percent of real estate holdings. By comparison, at the beginning of the nineteenth century, households in four of today's developed economies had precious metal holdings equal to less than 18 percent of their real estate holdings.[8] Moreover, this latter ratio declined for the next 100 years to less than 3 percent, as financial systems developed. With increased access to market-rate credit one would expect Indian families to be willing to shift some of their current real-denominated wealth holdings into similarly real-denominated housing investments. These kinds of potentially enormous portfolio shifts are overlooked by mortgage demand estimates that focus only on household income levels, compared to house costs. A similar analytical problem arises when analysts such as Grimes use estimates of how much households are willing to pay out of current income to consume housing services as renters, to predict how much of current income they would be willing to allocate to mortgage payments. This approach necessarily overlooks the savings motivation for housing demand. It will, as a result, overlook a source of demand that contributes to the observed high levels of house price-to-income ratios observed in many developing countries.

Because legal regulations eliminated the threat of rapid foreclosure in the event of a default, lenders in India have successfully used incentives and moral suasion outside of the legal system to ensure that borrowers honor their mortgage contracts. In particular, they have focused on borrowers' concerns with their reputations, often through the use of third-party guarantees, as a means to effect contract enforcement. Third-party guarantees are sought on almost all mortgage loans. The third party is always someone the borrower respects – an older colleague or a relative, for example. Like the borrower, the guarantor also has to submit a financial statement. The statement must show an ability to repay the loan in the event that the borrower cannot or will not do so. If loans are not repaid promptly the borrower is immediately notified. If the borrower's response is unsatisfactory, the threat of calling on the guarantor for repayment is raised, and ultimately carried out as a response to further recalcitrance on the borrower's part. If such follow-up still produces no response, legal action is initiated. Ultimately, neither the borrower nor the guarantor's rights are subverted by this way of inducing contract fulfillment. However, neither is the formal legal code used to provide the basis for effective contract governance. The value that the borrower is protecting by repaying is not the value of the house; it is the value of the borrower's reputation.

2.6 CONCLUSION

The role of better contract enforcement as a limiting factor on the growth of housing finance systems has been stressed here. Nevertheless, it is also clear that in some developing countries there is relatively little demand for housing finance. For instance, if a household wanted to spend a small portion of income on housing services (as might be the case in countries with very low *per capita* incomes), if land titles were also unclear, and the administrative costs of intermediation exceed say 4 percent, formal housing finance would probably not be in great demand. In this kind of environment, mutual organizations and nongovernmental organizations can be expected to be very effective, offering their members a way to share and reduce the administrative costs of intermediation. Even more important, such organizations can help develop credible contracts requiring that loans be repaid as long as the borrower is able to do so.

On the other hand, such pessimism does not apply to countries where the basic urban and financial infrastructure already exists. In most developing countries, which are attempting to liberalize and accelerate the development of the financial systems, the development of credible contracts can play an important role in improving both shelter conditions and the financial system. Mechanisms that allow long-term contracts to protect the interests of both savers and borrowers – such as fair but efficient foreclosure procedures and the appropriate type of mortgage instrument – can do much more than just contribute to a better-functioning housing market.

3 The Fiscal Policy Dimension

This chapter emphasizes the implicit fiscal dimension of housing polices. This perspective shows how a traditional public finance perspective on the rather modest levels of government spending in the sector is misleading. For understanding the government's role in the housing sector, it is less government's spending than implicit taxes and subsidies which are the major policy instruments. The chapter also presents evidence on how the sector has been affected by the way the world's more volatile financial environment has interacted with these implicit policies. Simple applications of a framework, which is developed more formally in Chapter 5, provide some insights into why policy-makers might undertake such approaches.

3.1 INTRODUCTION

In contrast to its importance as a source of capital formation and wealth, housing does not often figure heavily in the fiscal affairs of governments. As related in Chapter 1, the housing sector typically accounts for only about 2 percent of government expenditures. These expenditures also appear to be highly idiosyncratic. They are only weakly related to the rate or the level of economic development or urbanization.[1] Against this background, it is easy to conclude that government policy in the sector is of low priority, and is as likely to be dictated by cultural proclivities or politics as it is by economic factors. This view is incorrect. It stems from too narrow a measurement of the role of the government in the sector.

To understand how the housing sector functions, and to evaluate policies in this sector, the 'off-budget' operations of governments are far more important than traditional 'on-budget' expenditures. In fact, as the case studies of subsequent chapters show, these unmeasured transfers sometimes augment and sometimes offset the explicit transfers in budget documents. The result is that budget documents provide little information on a government's policy stance.

Because the implicit subsidies and taxes imposed on this sector are often the by-products of the pursuit of other policies it is difficult to generalize about the details of the role of the sector in the economy in a cross-country comparison. 'As a result, our discussion of the causes of our empirical results is stylized. We want to emphasize the types and rationales for policy-induced distortions rather than argue that such policies were uniformly pursued.

3.2   THE HOUSING SECTOR AND THE ECONOMY SINCE THE MID-1970s

During the 1970s a series of economic shocks jolted the world economic system, leading by the latter half of the decade to an environment characterized by high inflation and high and volatile, nominal and real interest rates.[2] These conditions added a significant new element of risk to saving and investment decisions. Perhaps as important, the new environment carried with it a new and largely unmeasured shift in the incentives generated by government policies. In the new environment, government financial and fiscal mechanisms, which in the past had permitted developing countries to accelerate the capital formation patterns, no longer produced the same results.

Financial institutions, in particular, have been dramatically affected by the changed environment. In many developing countries long-standing trends of increased financial deepening were first slowed and then reversed. For example, consider how the behavior of one frequently used measure of financial deepening, the ratio of $M2$ (broadly defined monetary holdings) to GDP, has changed in recent years.[3] Comparing this ratio for a sample of developing countries over the 1965–73 period to the 1973–85 period, we find that in the first period, growth in this trend was common. Financial deepening progressed broadly; less than 6 percent of the countries experienced a reduction in the ratio. In contrast, over the 1973–85 period more than 50 percent of the countries experienced a reduction in this ratio. In many developing economies financial intermediation contracted, sometimes very sharply.

Moreover, this simple measure of financial deepening tends to understate the scale of the disruptions of financial systems. Countries which, according to this measure, appear to be continuing the process of financial deepening have also experienced significant problems within their financial systems. India, for example, whose $M2$/GDP ratio had the sharpest percentage increase over the 1973–85 period, had a stagnating share of savings in financial assets and a commercial banking system whose financial position had deteriorated sharply since the mid-1970s.[4] As mentioned earlier, the profitability and solvency problems of financial institutions are significant and pervasive across developing countries.

Very high real borrowing rates, severe balance of payments' problems, and much higher inflationary 'taxes' on financial savings have made it less attractive for savers to provide funds for financial systems. In addition, government demands on this shrinking or stagnating financial base increased significantly. The cumulative result has been increasing competition for a relatively (and sometimes absolutely) smaller pool of funds.[5] For borrowers who have less favored access to credit markets, such as households, the result has been less credit.

There has long been a view in development economics that these kinds of financial system problems will result in disintermediation from financial systems and more investment in speculative assets such as housing as 'unproductive' inflation hedges, see Taylor (1981). Hence, the changed environment could have induced more, rather than less, housing investment. However, unlike most other substitutes for financial assets, housing investments are so large and indivisible that purchasing often requires finance, and finance has been limited. In addition, for those who can find and afford such financing there are often other regulations – such as rent control – which make it preferable to leave housing units vacant rather than to rent them to those who could afford to rent but not to buy. Finally, in many developing countries institutional development is such that the high costs of clear and enforceable titles discourage such investment.

In the end, however, we do not know whether the shift out of financial assets of the 1980s was likely to lead to more or less housing investment. Whether housing's characteristics are such that investors are constrained from making such investments, is ultimately an empirical question which we have analyzed in an appendix to this chapter.

The estimated regression equations consider: (1) housing investment (RES) as a share of GDP; and (2) as a share of gross fixed capital formation (GFCF). They are a functional form previously employed by Burns and Grebler (1976). Similar to their findings, the estimated equations indicate that across countries housing demand is income elastic over a wide range of incomes. As countries develop, the share of GDP allocated to housing rises until a country reaches a relatively high income status.

Regressions are estimated for two periods – one centered in the mid-1970s, the other centered in the early 1980s. Figures 3.1 and 3.2 present the results of the estimated regression equations from the appendix to this chapter. They indicate downward shifts in housing investment at every level of GDP *per capita*. In the case of housing investment to GDP (shown in Figure 3.1) the shift downward varies from about 0.4 percentage points at a per capita GDP of $1 000 per year in US$1 981 (11 percent of the estimated mid-1970 value of *RES/GDP* at $1 000) to a maximum of about 1.8 percentage points at a per capita income of $9 800 (26 percent of the estimated mid-1970 value of *RES/GDP* at $9 800). In the case of housing investment to GFCF, the downward shift varies from about 2.9 percentage points at GDP *per capita* of $1 000 to about 4.9 percentage points at GDP *per capita* of $9 300 per year. Throughout the range of GDP *per capita*, there is a downward shift of about 17 percent of the estimated mid-1970 value of *RES/GFCF*. The observed shifts in housing investment indicate that housing declined as a proportion of GDP, and that countries' investment portfolios underwent a shift away from housing during the latter half of the 1970s.

Clearly, the causes and consequences of such shifts in individual countries depend upon the specific policies pursued, as well as on macroeconomic performance. In addition, the complexity of the mechanisms by which such effects are propagated is considerable. However, it is important to note that it is unlikely that the disruption in income growth was the source of the fall in housing investment. This source of instability can be ignored because of another empirical regularity of housing demand, documented for developed countries by Mayo (1985b), and for developing countries by Malpezzi and Mayo (1987a). The regularity is: housing demand is highly income-

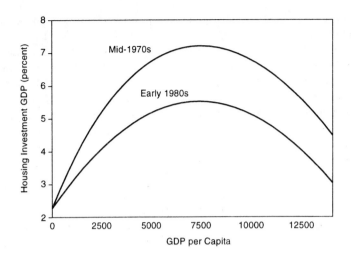

Figure 3.1   Housing investment and GDP

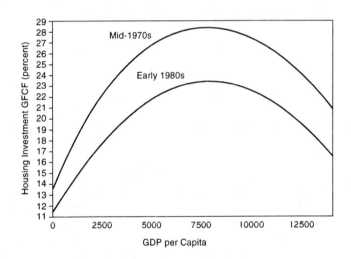

Source: R. Buckley and S. Mayo (1989).

Figure 3.2   Housing investment and capital formation

inelastic over time in one country, as opposed to across countries at a point in time. Accordingly, if housing demand moves in sympathy with, but at a slower rate than income, an income reduction would increase the share of GDP allocated to housing. Hence, the observed pattern must be generated by changes in financial conditions – that is, changes in interest rates and credit conditions.

While we are agnostic as to which financial channel propagated the reduction, we are not agnostic about the effects of the policies that could be expected to lead to such a result. Many of these policies are costly for both the economy and the sector. In addition, because they are policy-induced they are, by definition, more amenable to change. Consequently, we first consider why these kinds of policies may be pursued, and then we focus on the kinds of broader economic effects they can induce.

3.3 THE INTERACTION OF REGULATORY REGIMES WITH THE CHANGING ECONOMIC ENVIRONMENT: IMPLICATIONS FOR HOUSING INVESTMENTS

Our perspective on the broad relationship between regulatory policy and the housing market follows the work of Penner and Silber (1973) and is described more formally in Chapter 5. It focuses on housing as an asset, and the effects of regulations and controls on the substitutability between assets. In this approach, one extreme is represented by highly developed economic systems in which markets rely completely on interest rates to allocate access to credit. The regulatory systems of these economies could be characterized as having a perfectly elastic supply of credit for every sector at the market rate of interest. In this case, all credit instruments are perfect substitutes. At the other extreme are economic and formal financial systems that are more representative of developing countries. These systems rely exclusively on quantity controls to allocate credit and/or resources. The supply of formal credit to a particular sector can be characterized as perfectly interest-rate inelastic at a level determined by policy-makers. There is no possibility of substitution between financial assets.

In the latter kind of system, if the quantity of mortgage credit contracts and interest rates are not permitted to increase, households are unable to borrow as much as they want. Increasing the quantity of mortgage credit supplied at market interest rates would reduce the resulting disequilibrium. However, this could only be accomplished by bidding resources away from another sector. In most developing economies, even before the contractions in financial deepening, such bidding for resources by households was prevented by regulatory policies. Instead of allowing competition for funds, financial policies in most countries attempted to direct credit to what were thought to be high pay-off investments. For example, until the 1980s, India's highly centralized credit system effectively fixed the supply of formal finance for the housing sector at a low, interest insensitive level. The policy rationale was that housing and infrastructure should not be allowed to bid resources away from other more productive sectors.

Another possible rationale for reliance on quantity-controlled financial systems is that such systems can make the economy less sensitive to real-side economic shocks, for example, shocks that shift the demand for credit curve. In controlled systems, reductions in demand (due, for example, to a fall in income) are more likely to be reflected in price reductions than in changes in output. For many low-income economies that are subject to real-side economic risks, this use of controls can help distribute economy-wide risks (for example, that rains arrive). However, while this type of system may have been effective in allocating the risks of relative price changes, it was far less effective in dealing with financial disturbances that shift the credit supply curve.[6] As a result, changes in financial conditions can have a greater effect on output than they would in a less regulated economy. In addition, the sectors most acutely affected are those that are most reliant on finance, such as housing and infrastructure investments.

A final rationale for the reliance on quantity-controlled financial systems stems from the 'fine-tuning' macro-management perspectives. This view has long played a part in macroeconomic management policy in both developed and developing countries. In more developed economies, it takes the form of an argument that segmentation and control over the credit markets make macroeconomic management easier (see Modigliani, 1977). According to this line of argument, portfolio restrictions on mortgage lenders, for example, could be used to 'cool the economy off' more easily. Interest rate ceilings on the deposits offered by mortgage lenders would cause funds to be drained from these institutions whenever market interest rates increased. The result would be that investment in the housing sector would fall off sharply as mortgage borrowers were rationed out of the capital markets. Changes in availability, rather than price, of credit would be the channel through which monetary policy would reduce both housing and aggregate demand. Housing investment, according to this approach, serves as the cyclical handmaiden of stabilization policy. Cyclical cutbacks in housing expenditures may be more severe, but they should also be relatively short-lived. The 'credit crunches' that generated housing production cycles have been argued to have played such 'a constructive role' in the US (see Harberger, 1970).

There are two problems with relying on this market-segmentation policy perspective to shape policies in developing countries. First, while such controls may help protect against the risks of relative price changes, they are less effective when risks from the monetary side of the economy increase. These latter risks have increased throughout the world. Second, even if one were to subscribe to a 'fine-tuning' rationale for a quantity control system, in many countries the continual rationing out of residual borrowers cannot be described as cyclical. Secular reductions in the share of credit available to the housing sector of the sort that have occurred have very different effects on the economy than do short-term cyclical reductions.

3.4 SOME EXAMPLES OF BROADER CONSEQUENCES OF IMPLICIT FISCAL POLICIES: POLAND

In a world of stable interest rates and low inflation, it is not difficult to understand why a macroeconomic planner might favor the kinds of policies that lead to a reduced level of housing investment. Now consider how this kind of perspective was implemented in a world of higher and more volatile inflation.

For example, consider the case of a government using interest-rate policies and its credit allocation powers to make financial institutions hold government debt at below market interest rates. Such a policy can lower the government's accounting costs of borrowing. A policy that places restrictions on access to credit effectively causes the supply curve on mortgage credit to shift to the left as the government 'crowds out' other borrowers. No explicit change in government tax or expenditure policy is associated with the policy. However, because households cannot issue mortgages against their largest and collaterally safest asset, they are confronted with a higher market interest rate for borrowing. Because the available credit is allocated to priority sectors there is also a reduced quantity of mortgage credit supplied by the formal sector.

Finally, because mortgages are substitutes for other means of borrowing, housing is not the only asset affected by the reduced supply of mortgage credit. All non-government borrowers face a higher real cost of borrowing even if interest rate ceilings obscure this effect. For most households this policy-induced, higher effective mortgage-interest-rate means a higher effective opportunity cost for discounting their future earnings. As a result, the policy also causes the present value of most households' wealth to be reduced.

Other policies can lower the value of the new housing because, for example, they limit the financing available for the accompanying infrastructure investment. These policies have the effect of shifting the mortgage demand function down, thereby reducing housing investment. But in this case, they may bid up the demand and prices of existing properties that already have infrastructure. Typical policies could easily be imagined that have similar price effects on the housing and asset markets. Clearly a variety of government policies exist, many of which are 'off the books', that can and do have major influences on the sector and the economy. Even under stable economic conditions, policies such as directed credit and the rationing of infrastructure investments can have significant effects. In times of high and unstable real borrowing rates, high and volatile inflation, and steeply negative real deposit-rates, the effects of such policies are likely to be more drastic for many long-term borrowers.

A better sense of the nature and magnitude of the costs of such shifts can be achieved by considering specific examples. Part II of the book presents a number of case studies that simplify some very complicated policies and behavioral responses. Here a brief discussion of one case, Poland, demonstrates that under what we think are conservative assumptions, unbudgeted housing and financial policies have had very disruptive consequences for the sector and the economy. The estimates of impact may lack the precision of

traditional budgetary accounting measures. Nevertheless, they illustrate some of the notions necessary for understanding the way in
which government policy affects the housing sector outside of traditional fiscal instruments.

The Polish example provides an explanation for the simultaneous
existence of enormous levels of housing subsidy – 13 percent of
government budget outlays – and housing shortage. According to
budgetary figures it appears that too much is going into the sector:
Poland provides one of the world's highest levels of government
housing expenditures. An obvious policy response to these figures
would be the recommendation that fewer resources should be allocated to the housing sector, exactly the opposite position implied
by measures of housing shortage. These conclusions, however, are
reversed when economic, rather than simple budget accounting
concepts, are used to evaluate the effects of government policy. As
Mayo and Stein (1995) show, large government transfers to the sector
were more than offset by other government regulatory policies. Housing
waiting lists of many years have been and continue to be the norm.
Clearly, in Poland the scale of measured government expenditures
on housing is a very misleading indicator of the effects of government policy on the sector.

3.5   CONCLUSION

The shifts in the world economy during the debt crisis of the 1980s
created a situation of declining investment in housing and urban
infrastructure. The transition from socialism in the 1990s produced
a similar reduction in housing investments. In many cases these drops
have been dramatic. All too often the decline in economic activity
within these sectors has been seen as an unfortunate, but necessary,
consequence of the need to adjust to the difficult external economic
conditions that have characterized the past 15 years. No doubt in
many cases a cyclical reduction in housing investment was very
helpful in achieving macro-stability. However, in many cases policies have been pursued that have inadvertently led to deliberate
suppression of these highly visible non-tradable goods.

These effects occur, largely because of the enormous leverage that
governments can exert on incentives within the housing sector. The

extremely long life of housing means that the present value of current policies can have magnified effects in both the housing sector and credit markets. To a considerable degree it is because of the durability of housing that policy regarding it can have such major impacts. When policies affect the price of this asset and the access to credit necessary to finance it, economy-wide incentives can shift dramatically, affecting consumption, savings, investment, and other major economic aggregates.

In many countries, neglect of the macroeconomic implications of housing-oriented policies has undoubtedly deepened their economic crises. On the other hand, housing policy reform can often play a fundamental role in easing the current economic problems of developing countries. The balance sheet effects, as well as income statements, of such long-lived policies should be analyzed. Indeed, to confine policy analysis to a narrow examination of the benefits and costs of government 'income statements', that is, expenditure programs for housing, is to risk being deceived by 'fiscal illusion'. Such a perspective may miss the most important impacts of government policy.

3.6 APPENDIX

Housing Investment and the Level of Development

We examine here two measures of the level of economic activity of the housing sector: (1) the ratio of housing investment to GDP, and (2) the ratio of housing investment to gross fixed capital formation (GFCF). The former of these two relationships has been analyzed by Burns and Grebler (1976) Renaud (1980) and others for periods up to and including the early 1970s. This research revealed a consistent and quite stable relationship between the ratio of housing investment and GDP with GDP *per capita*: the share of housing investment in GDP first increasing with levels of GDP *per capita* (up to a level of about US$8 000 in 1981) and then declining as *per capita* GDP continued to increase.

To gauge the impact of the economic conditions of the period since the late 1970s on these relationships, data were collected for about 50 developed and developing countries for two periods – the mid-1970s (centered on 1976 for most countries in the sample) and the early 1980s (centered on 1981 for most countries in the sample). Two regression equations were estimated for each period with the dependent variables defined as follows:

(1) *RES/GDP* = the ratio of housing investment to GDP
(2) *RES/GFCF* = the ratio of housing investment to GFCF

and with two independent variables, GDP *per capita* and GDP *per capita* squared. The functional form of these equations follows the specification of Burns and Grebler (1976), although it does not include some other variables they included, such as the rate of population growth and the relative rate of population growth in urban areas and the entire country. These latter variables were not included here because they were not expected to have changed much over a five-year period, and because their exclusion would certainly have had only a negligible impact on any test of the shift in regression parameters from the mid-1970s to the early 1980s. The data are from *Compendium of Human Settlements Statistics*, United Nations, New York, 1985.

Hypotheses concerning the two estimated relationships are as follows:

• The relationship between housing investment and GDP should be similar in both time-periods with *RES/GDP* first rising and then falling with GDP *per capita*; however:
• For given levels of GDP *per capita*, it is expected that there will be lower levels of *RES/GDP* in the latter time period.
• The relationship between housing's share of GFCF and GDP *per capita* is expected to exhibit a similar relationship to GDP as that between housing investment and GDP *per capita*, first rising and then falling with GDP *per capita*, however,
• For given levels of GDP *per capita* it is expected that there will be lower levels of *RES/GFCF* in the latter time period.

Before presenting the results of the regression equations, it is useful to consider shifts in the two dependent variables between the two time-periods. In the mid-1970s the average ratios of housing investment to GDP and housing investment to GFCF were respectively 7.2 percent and 28.3 percent for the sample of countries investigated. By the early 1980s these ratios had fallen to 5.5 percent and 23.4 percent, respectively. Thus, on average, housing investment's share of GDP and its share of capital formation had fallen significantly in just a five-year period. The gross declines in housing investment are borne out by the results of regression models of the two time-periods which are as follows:

Mid-1970s

$$RES/GDP = 2.236 + 0.001239 \text{ GDP} - 7.719* \ 10^{-8} \text{ GDP}^2$$
$$R^2c = 0.56 \ (0.000192) \ (1.446* \ 10^{-8})$$

$$RES/GFCF = 13.739 + 0.003501 \text{ GDP} - 2.107* \ 10^{-7} \text{ GDP}^1$$
$$R^2c = 0.38 \ (0.000816) \ (6.138* \ 10^{-8})$$

Early 1980s

RES/GDP = 2.203 + 0.000885 GDP − 5.919* 10^{-8} GDP^2

R^2c = 0.28 (0.000240) (1.859* 10^{-8})

$RES/GFCF$ = 11.313 + 0.002961 GDP − 1.816* 10^{-7} GDP^2

R^2c = 0.24 (0.000991) (7.666* 10^{-8})

Standard errors are in parentheses. All coefficients are significant at or above the .05 level.

4 The Real Sector Dimension

4.1 INTRODUCTION

The benefits of market economies over centrally-planned economies stem from economic agents freely responding to prices that better reflect real social costs. The liberalization of prices to reflect true economic scarcity is a top priority for policy-makers in the previously centrally-planned economies (PCPEs) for two reasons. First, rents were one of the most distorted of all prices, owing to the status of housing as a social (as opposed to economic) good.[1] Increasing rents will generate substantial efficiency gains in reallocating the existing stock (Daniel and Semjen, 1987 and Tolley, 1991). Second, well-functioning housing markets are an essential precondition for developing a market-based economy. For example, labor-market efficiency would be enhanced through vastly improved household mobility (Blanchard et al., 1991), and the efficiency of capital accumulation and allocation would be improved by funding entrepreneurial effort via borrowing against the largest simple form of wealth – homeowner equity (Newberry, 1992).

Conversion of the housing sector is said to be high on the list of reform-minded governments, as well as international agencies.[2] Nonetheless, progress to date has been slow, and privatization initiatives have often stalled, and in some countries, such as China, it will be phased in over several decades.[3]

Blanchard et al. (1991, pp. 36–9) make the case for rapid privatization of state assets through giveaways, whereas McKinnon (1991) presents the case for 'going slow'. Our conclusion is identical with that of Blanchard et al.: the arguments against rapid housing privatization 'are ill thought-out'.

Two types of arguments have been made for not privatizing rapidly. First, the existing housing stock is unaffordable in private ownership. Second, governments cannot afford to forego the revenue from the housing stock. Both are based on a partial analysis of how central planning distorted rents, ignoring its simultaneous distortions to household income and wealth. In market economies, housing-affordability arguments always reduce to some households having relatively less income than others; hence, housing subsidies are introduced as an in-kind transfer. This household-specific argument cannot be extended to the total population of an economy *vis-à-vis* its existing housing stock. While enormous subsidies are provided to renters in the PCPEs, the full cost of these subsidies is currently being paid by the existing population. The affordability argument does not recognize that the existing stock of housing was financed out of past taxes and is in effect already paid for. Giving households their housing units would simply be giving them ownership-in-exchange rights to housing units over which they already exercise ownership-in-use rights.

The second argument is that governments need to retain the housing stock because it will generate either an ample stream of revenues or a large lump sum when sold at market prices.[4] This argument has been made most forcefully by Tideman (1994), the originator of a 'Dear Mr Gorbachev Letter'. This letter, which was signed by a number of prominent American economists, including Nobel Prize winners Tobin and Solow, urged Gorbachev not to privatize land-holdings in the process of reform. The letter was distributed widely in the former Soviet Union.

Newly elected governments need to develop stable revenue sources, retaining ownership of even the land under the existing public housing stock will not do so. Serious principal – agent problems have emerged as new mayors become the stewards of extensive local government asset-holdings, see Alm and Buckley (1994). In addition, as shown by Renaud (1991), the current operation of public housing loses money in all the PCPEs. Giving such assets away would increase government revenues even if no taxes on private-housing returns or capital were collected. This conclusion is only altered slightly by proposed rent increases, which in most cases would increase the present value of net rents to less than 20 percent of reproduction cost, or less than the present value of the tax revenue the government would be expected to collect from private owners.

Neither is the conclusion altered fundamentally by apparent sales of some properties at prices significantly above fundamental value.

Such sales would either shrink the domestically-occupied housing stock or fuel inflation. Moreover, the resultant perception that rents are unaffordable stifles serious reform. Preventing such sales is another argument for, not against, housing giveaways.

The persistent misconception that the housing stock has large fundamental value relates to the gap between the level of subsidized administered rents and long-run equilibrium free-market rents. Of course, if rents were at unsubsidized free-market levels, fundamental value would be substantial. But rents cannot get to such levels unless the income funding current subsidies is returned to the population. As a result, all analyses of reform have recommended rent and wage increases as a necessary first step.

At this point we need to emphasis the *two* sources of subsidies in existing rents and the reforms necessary to restore demand to free-market levels. As is well known (Kornai, 1990; and Blanchard *et al.*, 1991), socialist economies generally repressed wages and implicitly 'taxed' business income at rates of 100 percent or more. This in effect, amounts to an income tax on wages. The current implicit wage income tax in the PCPEs funds numerous subsidies, including the ongoing operating subsidies for housing.[5]

While rents have risen sufficiently to cover operating costs in a number of countries (Kingsley and Struyk, 1992), the gap between long-run equilibrium and administered rents is still huge. This gap represents the second subsidy, the return on capital from past housing investments. Households financed capital subsidies for past investments with 'forced savings' through the wage repression mechanism just described. Rents can be raised to free market levels only if the 'dividends' from investment in the existing housing stock are restored to household income.

The restoration should not be provided through wage reform (that is, be tied to the number of hours worked) because doing so would distort labor markets and reduce international competitiveness. Rather, the dividend income should be distributed, which is fiscally equivalent to giving away the existing housing stock. Identification of the state's housing dividend as the major source of current, subsidized rent levels explains the seeming dichotomy between the low fundamental (rental) value of public housing and the perceived high market value (which includes the present value of future dividends).

While the dividend could be paid either in one lump sum or over time, we strongly advocate the one-time special dividend. As Olsen (1982) argues, the fall of communism offers policy-makers a unique but fleeting opportunity to break the existing institutional, political obstacles by irretrievably giving away the housing stock. A continuing dividend keeps the housing stock in the hands of the government and is all too easy to cancel at some future date.

Restoring effective demand is not the only condition necessary for robust private-housing markets. Liberalizing prices while production is still controlled by state monopolies does not necessarily produce a supply response. The primary focus of this chapter, however, is the need to restore housing-market demand, assuming that the supply-side reforms described in Renaud (1991) are implemented. More specifically, the central question for rapid housing privatization concerns the distribution of the dividend from the existing housing stock, rather than the much thornier wage- and rent-level questions that have been the emphasis of all other studies. From this it follows that policy should focus on developing an equitable formula for giving away the vast majority of the housing stock, while implementing all supply reforms (breaking up inefficient state monopolies, developing property rights, and so on).

The remainder of this chapter is divided into four sections. Section 4.2 describes the working of real-estate markets in market economies. Section 4.3 identifies the distortions introduced by central planning, and section 4.4 discusses alternative transitions to a free real-estate market. The final section summarizes the paper.

4.2 REAL-ESTATE SECTOR IN MARKET ECONOMIES

A discussion of real-estate markets in market economies is best presented in two parts: (1) the long-run equilibrium and (2) the adjustment from a disequilibrium to the equilibrium.

Long-Run Equilibrium

In full equilibrium, net (of operating expenses) rent equals the rental or user cost (uc), the quantity of space equals the demand for it, and the value of the space equals its replacement cost. Measuring the user cost as the sum of the financing cost (real after-tax financing rate) and depreciation, *grossed up by unity* less the tax rate, after-tax net (of operating expenses) rents must cover the financing cost and depreciation. Solving this relation for the pretax gross rental rate:

$$Pr/RC = (fin + depr)/(1-\tau) + oper/RC \qquad (4.1)$$

where *Pr* is the price of (gross rent on) a unit of space, *RC* is the replacement cost of a unit of space, *fin* is the real after-tax financing rate, *depr* is the depreciation rate, *oper* is operating expenses (utilities and maintenance) per unit space, and r is the rate at which rents, less operating expenses are taxed.

In general, value (*V*) equals the present value of expected future after-tax net rental income. But in equilibrium, where these future rents are expected future user costs, new construction exactly earns normal profits and the real asset value of a unit of space equals its replacement cost:

$$V = RC \qquad (4.2)$$

In a well-functioning market economy, demand and supply are equal because price adjusts to bring demand into line with the existing stock. We express the demand for space as a positive function of income (*Y*) and a negative function of the price (rent) of space relative to the price of other goods (*Pr/Po*) and equate demand (*D*) to the existing supply or *Q*:

$$D = D(Y, Pr/RCPo) = Q \qquad (4.3)$$

We abstract here from vacancy rates. With vacancies, we would convert *Pr* to an effective rent and *Q* to an effective quantity (would multiply both by one less the vacancy rate), and, in disequilibrium, we would allow for differences between the actual and 'natural' vacancy rates.

Figure 4.1 describes the rental market for space. The solid schedules describe full equilibrium; the quantity of space is such that demand and supply are equated at $(Pr - oper)/R = uc$ (in which case $V = RC$). Excess demand is illustrated by the dashed demand schedule,

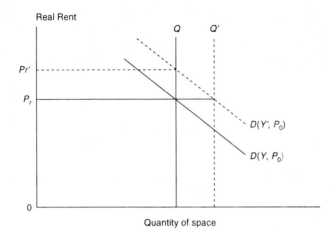

Figure 4.1   Rental market in a market economy

where $Y' > Y$ and thus $Pr' > Pr$. In this situation, value exceeds replacement cost and new construction will be induced until Q rises to Q' and full equilibrium again exists, as we shall now explain.

Adjustment to Equilibrium

Three more equations are needed to capture the essence of the adjustment process. First, we express net construction (C) as a positive function for the value/replacement-cost ratio:

$$C = C(V/RC) \qquad (4.4)$$

With V/RC exceeding unity, new space can be sold for more than the cost of producing it. Thus construction in excess of depreciation will occur. With V/RC less than unity, construction will be less than depreciation. In fact, if the value of space in this use is below the value in an alternative use by more than the cost of conversion, conversion to the alternative use will occur. To capture the impacts of net construction and net conversions ($CONV$) out of the stock, we express the stock in period t in terms of the previous period stock and net construction and conversions (both between $t - 1$ and t):

$$Q_t = Q_{t-1} + C - CONV \tag{4.5}$$

The last, and probably most important relationship for what follows, is the determination of fundamental value, the present value of expected future, net real-rental income. Assuming that the operating expense ratio, tax rate, depreciation rate and financing rate are constant, Equation (4.6) illustrates three fundamental points. First, and most obvious, valuation requires market participants to make long-term forecasts of real rents. Second, if rents only cover operating costs (and are expected to do so 'forever'), then value is zero. Third, if the market is in full equilibrium, market rents equal their long-run equilibrium value $(Pr\text{-}oper)/RC = (fin + depr)/(1 - \tau))$ and $V = RC$.

Equation (4.6) is usefully rewritten as

$$V = (1 - PVBERI)RC \tag{4.6a}$$

where *PVBERI* is the present value of expected below equilibrium rental income.

Numerous 'disturbances' can change fundamental value: changes in *uc* (in *fin*, τ or *oper*), in *RC* (real labor costs, production technologies) or in the expected path of the *Pr*'s (owing, possibly, to changes in government policies). As a general rule, we would expect changes in these variables over any short period to be small (costs and technologies generally change slowly) or to be temporary in nature (real after-tax interest rates rising and then cycling back down). Combined with a fairly rapid production response, real value would not fluctuate sharply.

The 1980s provided an exception to this rule in the United States. Owing to a breakdown in prudent lending practices, an unprecedented commercial building boom occurred. Real office-market rents were halved, and real fundamental value fell by over a third, relative to replacement cost, Hendershott and Kane (1992). This 'lending-frenzy' is estimated to have reduced commercial real-estate values by $250 to $300 billion dollars and to have wasted about $125 billion of economic resources. The frenzy is largely attributable to erroneous government regulatory and private-sector lending practices.

The recent US experience should be a warning to countries reforming their real-estate sectors. Even in a purportedly stable market economy, lending and building errors of enormous magnitude can occur. The potential for such errors in economies with highly distorted real-estate markets must be far greater. And with tenuous macroeconomic stability, the social as well as economic costs of such errors would be multiplied many times over.

4.3 THE REAL-ESTATE SECTOR IN CENTRALLY-PLANNED ECONOMIES

Real-estate sectors in centrally-planned economies functioned far differently than those in market economies. Construction was subsidized, interest rate and rent subsidies were given for owners and renters, respectively, wages were repressed ('taxed') to fund the subsidies, and exchange was often proscribed or discouraged. We begin by describing how these policies distort markets and then discuss whether the PCPEs have over- or under-invested in housing during the last 45 years.

The Controlled Housing Sector of a PCPE

Construction costs in the PCPEs were previously directly lowered by four 'capital' subsidies: land was provided for residential use by the state at little or no cost; the price of labor and materials contained substantial subsidies; direct grants from the state budget were provided to finance construction of both owner-occupied housing and state-cooperative developments; and long-term mortgage financing for cooperative and owner-occupied housing was provided at below-market rates. There were also ongoing 'operating' subsidies: utility rates (central heating, electricity, water and sewer, gas, and trash collection) were set below economic-scarcity value, and state-owned companies typically provided upkeep and maintenance of the housing stock at administered prices.

The PCPEs raised revenues by suppressing wages well below productivity and 'taxing' enterprise profits. The tax revenues financing operating subsidies can be described as 'transfers', whereas the tax revenues subsidizing capital represent 'investments' in the state-owned housing stock. The tax was broadly based, but housing investments were made in discrete intervals. At any point in time, the tax on household income to fund capital subsidies was the implicit failure to pay 'market' dividends on the existing housing stock (that is, the implicit tax rate on housing dividends was 100 percent).

With α and β, respectively, of replacement-cost capital and current operating costs being subsidized, the total income suppression (SUP) necessary to fund all housing subsidies today is:

$$SUP = (Pr - Pr^c)Q = [\alpha finRC/(1-\tau) + \beta oper]Q \qquad (4.7)$$

where $Pr - Pr^c$, the difference between market and controlled rents, is the rental subsidy per unit housing and Q is the total quantity of (state owned) housing space. The current dividend income missing from household income is $\alpha[finRC/(1-\tau)]Q$, and the wage tax is $\beta operQ$. Current household income is reduced by both the lack of dividends and the wage suppression.

The present value of the expected missing after-tax dividend income is the wealth (homeowner equity) missing from PCPE household balance sheets. To understand how crucial homeowner equity generally is to the 'affordability' of market rents, consider the following. During the period of high interest rates in the US in the late 1970s, housing-market analysts concluded that, based on current prices and interest rates, and ignoring substantial homeowner equity, only about 10 percent of homeowners could afford the houses they lived in. This percentage would likely be even lower at the higher real interest rates and production costs characterizing the PCPEs. That is, without homeowner equity, the vast majority of PCPE households will not be able to afford their current housing.

Figure 4.2 illustrates how a real-estate market so controlled would deviate from a free market. With low rents, excess demand and a queue result: the income suppression reduces the demand for all goods and services, but all of the income is used to fund rent reductions. The queues are perhaps the most damaging consequence of the controlled market. Households are assigned a particular unit and are effectively prohibited from moving. That is, the existing housing stock is inefficiently allocated among households, and households are sub-optimally distributed geographically relative to their job locations. Moreover, effectively zero household mobility greatly undermines attempts at industrial restructuring.[6]

These subsidies result in huge differences between rents for con-

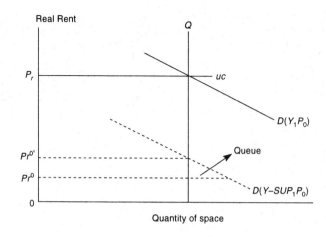

Figure 4.2 Rental market in a controlled economy

trolled (residential) and uncontrolled (commercial) real estate. The result is the development of 'gray markets' for illegal conversions to alternative uses. Thus the distortions in residential markets spill over into other real-estate markets.

Housing-market distortions also result in hoarding and an inefficient allocation of housing. Chapter 9 shows that the gains from permitting a market to reshuffle the entitlements to the existing stock of housing are equivalent to an increase in housing services generated by a year of production. These potentially large efficiency gains, however, require market prices to facilitate reallocation of the stock among households, to encourage renovation activity, and to provide proper signals for new construction.

The involuntary taxes to finance housing-demand place the state in the position of a price-insensitive monopoly developer. Kingsley and Maxiam (1992) estimate that real supply costs in the Czech Republic exceed competitive supply costs by 40 percent. We suspect even greater resource misuse in the former Soviet Republic, where price distortions were larger.

Over- or Under-Investment in Housing?

The conventional wisdom is that the cumulative effect of a half-century or more of planning and administrative allocation of housing has resulted in substantial under-investment in housing (Renaud, 1991). If this were the case, then demand, after the return of the housing stock to households, would exceed the existing stock at $Pr = uc$, and market rents would rise above uc. Value would exceed replacement cost, and new construction would be forthcoming, assuming a liberalized housing-supply sector. Because this response would take time, the economy would be at point A in Figure 4.3.

On the other hand, while shortages are expected at the low administered rent, increases in rent to the long-run equilibrium level could easily create an excess supply. Recall that the share of investment demand allocated to *all* consumer goods was low in most PCPEs relative to market economies. That is, after removal of rent subsidies these economies could be at point B in Figure 4.3, and little construction would be expected for many years.

We would anticipate that some local markets would be represented by point A and others by point B. However, several reasons lead one to doubt that the pre-reform state of disequilibrium is generally one of shortage. First, data on the PCPE shares of investment in housing are difficult to sort out and compare with those from market economies. Prell (1989), for example, argues that the post World War II growth of housing production in the Soviet Union was 'considerable' and almost twice as high as estimates made in the west. Similarly, Alexeev *et al.* (1991) show that during the 1957–64 period Soviet housing production *per capita* was the highest in the world, and the World Bank study of housing policy in Hungary indicates that during the 1970s Hungary was probably the world's leading producer of housing on a *per capita* basis. Finally, Goldsmith's (1985) data indicate that Soviet and Hungarian levels of housing assets – the only two PCPEs for whom there are such data – as a share of wealth are higher than many market economies.

Second, while the share of savings directed to nonresidential investments may have been higher than for market economies (see Kornai, 1986), the *value* of these investments probably was not (see Tanzi, 1991). World Bank estimates indicate that average returns on industrial investment for PCPEs over the last several decades were negative (Bleaney, 1988). Discounting the existing capital stock at a rate reflecting the real, marginal productivity of new capital would probably suggest that housing represents a proportionately greater share of wealth for PCPEs than for most market economies.

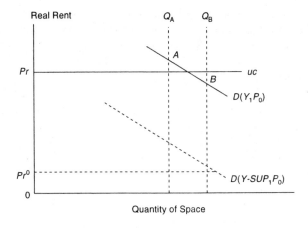

Figure 4.3 Rental market after 45 years of control

Third, even if housing is in short supply, there may well be a surplus of the generally disliked panel construction flats. The removal of all subsidies and a simultaneous boost in after-tax incomes (and housing wealth) could lead to an increase in demand for, and thus supply of, 'luxury' housing and a permanent surplus of panel flats.

We suspect that a substantial amount of renovation, repair and conversion work will meet the hurdle rate for new capital. But the share of GDP devoted to new housing construction projects that are viable at a 15 percent real cost of capital will probably be quite small, and the share devoted to panel construction produced by state monopolies will be negligible.[7]

4.4 TRANSITION TO A MARKET ECONOMY

The need to convert the housing sector is universally recognized. Disagreements arise regarding the optimal pattern and speed of adjustment, and the priority of housing over other reforms. While some advocate proceeding slowly on housing reform, we, like Tolley (1991), contend that speed is of the essence. There are three reasons for this. First, many of the gains from reform accrue only when reform is essentially complete. Second, gradual reform appears to be less likely politically. For example, during an election campaign in the summer of 1993, Hungary, which has been trying to raise rents to their full equilibrium for decades, froze nominal rents, meaning that real rents would decline. At almost the same time, and also shortly before a national election, Boris Yeltsin announced a similar deferment of a planned rent increase in Russia. Third, the major arguments against rapid reform are false: privatizing the housing stock will improve, not worsen the fiscal position of governments, and the housing stock can be privatized in an affordable and equitable manner.

This section addresses these arguments directly. We begin with an analysis of a very gradual transition to a free housing market, including the implications for real-estate values, and conclude that deeply subsidized housing is of virtually no value in the government's hands. We then describe the means to a rapid transition, and conclude with a discussion of equity concerns and political objections.

A Glacially Gradual Transition

If rents are raised, but not sufficiently to clear the market, virtually none of the benefits of housing reform are gained. Hoarding of large flats will continue (no efficiency gains from reallocation of the existing stock will occur), and labor-force mobility will not increase. Achieving market-clearing rents for the vast majority of markets is a minimal initial step. Referring back to Figure 4.2, the housing queue would be eliminated, and some government savings would be achieved as rents rose from Pr^c to $Pr^{c'}$. Generally, though, the rent increase and budget savings will be small because in most reforming economies few households can afford much higher rents. The fundamental problem is, of course, the income (and wealth) suppression. Until after-tax incomes or wealth are raised, few can afford to pay full-equilibrium rents.

How long will it take to get to full-equilibrium rents? Consider two cases. In the first, which approximates China, real rents are only one-tenth of full-equilibrium, and they will be raised by 10 percent a year. The adjustment takes 25 to 27 years, depending on the level of financing rates. In the second, which appears to approximate Romania, real rents are 25 percent of full-equilibrium (operating costs are covered), but real rents will be increased by only 5 percent a year. The adjustment is still 25 to 29 years.

Table 4.1 The value of real estate relative to replacement cost

	Rents = 10% of market		Rents = Operating costs	
	uc = .19	uc = .24	uc = .19	uc = .24
RC = 1.0	−.09	−.14	.23	.06
RC = 0.7	−.06	−.10	.16	.04

And just what is the housing stock currently worth under these scenarios? We can answer this question by using the valuation equations (4.6) and (4.6a), in which the ratio of value to replacement cost is related to the present value of below-equilibrium rents. Table 4.1 reports this ratio for the two slow transitions described above (real rents starting at 10 percent of market or covering operating expenses, respectively). The calculations are performed for two financing costs (high and low). In the first, $fin = 0.12$, $\tau = 0.2$, *oper* $= 0.06$ (0.03 each for maintenance and utilities), and *depr* $= 0.024$. Thus, from equation (4.1), $uc = 0.24$ and rents just covering operating costs initially equal a quarter of equilibrium rents (.06/.24). In the second, $fin = 0.08$, and thus $uc = 0.19$ and initial rents are about a third of equilibrium (0.06/0.19).

The values in the table are ratios to replacement cost, and those in the first row (RC = 1) are based on the further assumption that real construction costs have not changed since the housing was built. As can be seen, values are negative if real gross rents start out at only one tenth of equilibrium and rise at 10 percent per year. If rents initially cover operating costs and are expected to rise at 5 percent per annum in real terms, then value is positive, but equals only 6 percent of (depreciated) replacement cost in what we consider to be the more realistic high interest rate/user cost case. In the low real interest-rate scenario, value is almost a quarter of replacement cost.

The assumption of unchanged replacement cost seems inappropriate. Estimates by Kingsley and Maxiam (1992) suggest that the presubsidy production costs of state construction companies may be 40 percent greater than those of their private market counterparts. If this is true, the development of private construction companies will reduce replacement cost by 30 percent (0.4/1.4). In this case (row 2), value would be only 4 to 16 percent of original (depreciated) replacement cost, even when real rents initially cover operating costs and are expected to rise at 5 percent per year.

The values in Table 4.1 may seem low to some and certainly appear at odds with casual observation of isolated, high sales prices. The question is whether such observations support a go-slow privatization approach. We do not think so, and we explain by considering both motivations for, and specific types of sales.

One reason for high prices in some desirable markets is as a result of purchases by foreigners. Many are willing to pay close to reproduction-cost prices because they (1) have income and wealth (their income has not been suppressed) and (2) are not eligible for domestic rent subsidies. While such sales raise revenue, they also reduce the housing stock available for citizens. Whether the net deficit reduction – the declining available stock will increase pressure for subsidized production – is worth the net reduction in available housing is unclear.

Another reason for high prices is the conversion to other uses. Commercial rents in most PCPEs are unregulated, while supply has typically been restricted. Thus rents are often above, not below, equilibrium levels. With such rents, values above replacement cost are to be expected, and conversions from residential, though typically illegal, will follow. Here again, such conversions reduce the supply of housing for citizens.

Finally, governments might be able to generate sales prices above fundamental value by providing excess credit. However, not only is this inflationary, but the immediate revenue gain is likely to be offset by default losses in the future. Housing giveaways also avoid this problem.

A Rapid Transition

Two mechanisms for a rapid transition to a free-market housing system are an income supplement (rental housing allowances, such as those being employed in the former East Germany) and a wealth transfer (such as that implemented in Russia in 1992). Annual housing allowances would provide housing subsidies to the population that, in the aggregate, would equal the foregone annual regular dividend on the rental stock. Ownership vouchers would provide a one-time special dividend to households equal to the existing physical stock of government residential capital. Both mechanisms can be structured to reflect desired equity considerations.

While both mechanisms would entail substantial administrative, managerial, and other difficulties, the problems of the regular dividend mechanism are clearly more severe.

First, because there are currently no explicit housing dividends, the desired/needed level of housing allowances is unknown.[8] Second, the government as the single landlord would have the added practical difficulty of searching for the equilibrium rent, as well as the political problem of collecting the rents. This is a task governments throughout the world have shown little comparative advantage in doing. Third, the state would continue as the (inefficient) manager of the housing stock. In many respects, this path has been implicitly chosen by governments that do not privatize the stock. In these cases, existing tenants receive a 'pay out' equal to the maintenance support given by the public sector.

The surest and most efficient way to restore housing-market equilibrium without creating additional distortions during the transition, is to unwind totally the socialist housing legacy by eliminating all housing subsidies together with the taxes that finance them, and give away the existing stock.[9] With home-owner equity, market rents would then be affordable to most households. The transition would, of course, need to focus on creating an environment in which the giveaway would be accepted by tenants who, in some cases, are now paying very low rents.

A common objection to giving the stock away is the view that a valuable asset is being given up by an impoverished government. We have already addressed this objection, at least in part: if rents are below operating costs or expected to rise by less than 5 percent per year in real terms, then the housing 'asset' is really a liability. But what happens if rents equal operating expenses and are expected to rise by 5 percent per year in real terms, and in addition, the financing rate is only 8 percent? According to the calculation in Table 4.1, the stock is worth 0.23 of replacement cost. However, using the same 20 percent tax rate, the present value of tax revenue expected to be collected on earnings from a replacement-cost unit of the deregulated housing stock is even greater than 0.23. Calculating the present value of taxes from \$1 of stock as $\tau(uc - oper)/(fin + depr)$, we obtain 0.25 for any assumed level of the financing rate. Therefore, the deregulated housing stock is worth more to the government in private hands than the regulated housing stock is in the government's own hands.

Equity Concerns and Political Objections

A major concern with housing giveaways is the priority often extended to the existing tenant and thus the perpetuation of past inequities. This concern could, as mentioned earlier, be addressed through careful design of an ownership voucher plan. The vouchers would be distributed based on a politically determined formula. The state (or local government) could then set an initial price, in voucher units, for the housing stock. Vouchers would be issued for the entire stock. Then, an active secondary market could be created to facilitate housing-market adjustments.

The voucher scheme could, for example, allow those in the queue who have not yet received units to be compensated by those who have. In practice, an explicit 'vesting' scheme would be created *ex post*. Age (pensioners could be protected; they have, after all, had their wages suppressed longer than the young have), time in unit, and so on, are all issues politicians might address. Because the current housing system is inequitable to almost all and the voucher distribution scheme is infinitely malleable, equity concerns are not a legitimate obstacle to rapid market reforms.

We believe the political problems associated with this type of reform have been greatly aggravated by the previous focus on setting sales prices high and failing to consider a dividend distribution. The likelihood of a shrinking housing stock, owing to sales to foreigners and conversions to other uses, and the obvious advantage of those with accumulated liquid wealth raise legitimate concerns regarding eviction, foreclosure, and tenancy rights. Housing giveaways, on the other hand, would reduce these concerns by greatly increasing the affordability for most current tenants and thus reducing the political issue to the more manageable establishment of the appropriate social safety net.

Another reason for the delay in housing privatization is the perverse political incentives created by the transfer of the state housing stock, together with the liability for housing services, to local governments. Local governments have not yet developed alternative revenue sources, have no influence over wage reform, and are not taxed on liquidity overhang captured by asset sales. Consequently, they have an enormous incentive to maintain high sales prices and little incentive to speed reform (Alm and Buckley, 1994). The incentive mechanism for housing reform can be improved by the central government recouping proceeds from housing sales, adjusting revenue sharing, and providing the legal infrastructure that supports housing markets (Renaud, 1991).

Finally, we note that simply giving housing to existing tenants is no more inequitable than a glacially gradual increase in rents. In both cases those with better housing benefit equally, relative to those with worse housing. The efficiency gains that result from housing giveaways, however, make this a preferable alternative to gradual rent increase.

4.5 CONCLUSION

Transforming the housing sector to a market orientation ought to be a top priority of formerly socialist economies. This prioritization is appropriate because effectively-functioning housing markets would improve the utilization of the existing stock, and facilitate labor mobility, and thus productivity gains, in the industrial sector. It would also provide collateral to tap existing wealth for venture capital, as well as lower the cost of new housing construction. Despite these putative benefits, tangible progress toward housing-sector reform has, with a few notable exceptions, been very limited in most reforming countries, using as a benchmark the rent levels charged in public housing or the share of public housing stock that has been privatized.

From an analytical perspective, the failure to establish a well-functioning housing market stems primarily from two fundamental misconceptions. The first is that giving the housing stock away will erode the fiscal position of governments. The second is that the existing housing stock is unaffordable in private ownership.

The first misconception relates to valuing real estate. In many reforming economies, housing privatization decisions are being made at the local government level, and these cash constrained governments often expect asset sales to finance their operations. But real-estate values depend on expected future cash flows. Without bonafide rental reform, which cannot occur without distribution of the housing dividend, the housing stock in the PCPEs has trivial fundamental value (current cash flows are negative). While some sales can be achieved at prices above fundamental value, such sales either reduce the stock of housing available to citizens or fuel inflation. Giving away the housing stock is an excellent means to prevent such sales. Taxing the increased productivity at rates significantly below the 100 percent marginal rate implicit under state ownership improves the fiscal positions of both the government and households.

Rent-to-income ratios in the PCPEs are on the order of one-eighth of those in market economies. As is well recognized, these low ratios follow (in part) from a tax being placed on current wages to finance part of current rental operating costs. Not previously recognized is that the low ratios stem in larger part from a 100 percent implicit tax on the returns ('dividends') from past housing investments. Recognizing this tax is important for two reasons. First, without removal of the housing dividend tax, along with the wage tax, households will not be able to afford long-run equilibrium rents for at least a decade, and until they can, a well-functioning housing market will not exist. Second, understanding this tax helps clarify the very serious equity concerns that characterize and often obscure the privatization discussion.

While the return on the government-owned housing can be distributed as either an ongoing regular dividend or a one-time special dividend, the one-time giveaway is preferred. This method both assures the transition to a system in which housing services are allocated according to market signals and gets the government out of the housing management business. To not pay the special dividend could be to make a policy error of enormous proportions.

5 A Simple Theory of the Policy Dimensions of the Housing Sector

Although economic analysis of housing policy is complicated by legal and institutional considerations, the policy interest has generated a large and growing body of literature. Within this literature, however, no simple analytic framework is available to help in understanding the impacts and interactions of various policies and to explain how these impacts can change under different financial circumstances.

This chapter develops a simple, heuristic model of the housing market that can fill this gap. It borrows liberally from Hicks–Hansen *IS–LM* analysis and requires no more than simple algebra and very basic calculus to assess to qualitative impact of various policies. Its strength, however, is not in setting out comparative static signs, but in making assumptions that underline various policies more explicit and clarifying housing capital market relationships. The model is developed in the next section followed by a review of some housing market analyses and policies in light of the model's comparative statics.

5.1 A SIMPLE MODEL

If we assume that the flow of housing services, f, is proportional to the stock of owner-occupied housing, HS, that is, $f = KHS$, then because additions to the stock are small, KHS can be taken as fixed at each point in time, and demand determines the real net rental value of these services, R. Further, if we ignore depreciation, R can be related to the price of the stock of housing by the traditional user-cost of capital-pricing model $P_H = R/i_H$, where i_H is the real mortgage rate and P_H is the real price of housing. For a given R the

57

demand for housing is an inverse function of i_H, just as investment demand is an inverse function of 'the rate of interest'.

Besides the investment aspect of housing demand, demographic considerations, income or wealth, and government programs also play a role in housing expenditures. Just as aggregate demand in a macro-model is a function of consumption, investment, and government expenditure, so too are the expenditures for the stock of privately owned housing. For a given stock of housing, we can write a linear approximation of such of function in the following way:

$$H = B_0 + B_1 Y(1 - t) + B_2(HH - CH) - B_3 i_H - B_4 P_H = HS \quad (5.1)$$

where:

H = demand for housing services
P_H = real house prices
Y = real disposable income
t = income tax rate
HH = net household formation
CH = net public housing production[1]
B = impact coefficients (partial derivatives), and
HS = housing stock
i_H = real mortgage rate

In this form the demand for housing closely resembles the traditional *IS* expenditure function. One further adjustment must be made, however. Unlike the return on most other assets, the implicit rental value as well as most capital gains on owner-occupied units are not taxed at all. Because the return on most forms of capital is taxed on the nominal yield, or in many developing countries subject to interest-rate ceilings on deposits, the real after-tax rate is $(1 - t)i - \Theta$ where i is the nominal yield, and Θ the anticipated rate of inflation. The real return to taxed assets is thus a negative function of the anticipated rate of inflation. So instead of the usual assumption that the real rate of interest, in this case i_H, is neutral with respect to the anticipated rate of inflation, we adjusted i_H to take account of home-ownership's inflation-related tax advantage. Rewriting $(1 - t)i - \Theta$ as $(1 - t)(i - \Theta) - \Theta t$ helps make explicit the effect Θ and t have on alternative investments. In effect, then, higher rates of anticipated inflation can be viewed as lowering housing's cost of capital. To account for households rearranging the valuation of the assets in their portfolios in response to this change in relative yields, we change the next-to-last term in (5.1) to $B_3(i_H - \Theta t)$. With this adjustment the anticipated rate of inflation, Θ, still has no direct effect on the real mortgage rate, i_H, but increases in Θ reduce housing's relative cost of capital. Consequently, an increase in the anticipated rate of inflation causes a short-run increase in relative house prices unless the nominal mortgage rate is increased by $\Theta(1 + t)$.

So far we have specified a production function for housing services, $f = KHS$, an asset market equilibrium condition, $P_H = R/i_H$, and a housing market equilibrium condition. With these specifications we are able to solve for the pairs of house prices and housing stock that not only equilibrate the housing market, but also ensure that the valuation of housing compared to all other goods is such that all commodity markets are in equilibrium. In capital markets in which funds flowed costlessly to the highest yield, the mortgage rate would equal an exogenously determined cost of capital, C, and the impact of financial conditions would be reflected in the model. However, should there be imperfections in the capital markets which impede the flow of funds, as is the case is virtually all developing countries, then the supply of mortgage credit as well some notion of the degree of mortgage market segmentation must be embedded into the model.

We bring mortgage market considerations into the analysis by analogy to the money market in the traditional IS – LM approach. The following is an approximation of an equilibrium condition:[2]

$$M^S + e(i_H - C) = Z_0 + Z_1 Y(1 - t) + Z_2(HH - CH)$$
$$- Z_3 i_H + Z_4 P_H \qquad (5.2)$$

where

M^S = An exogenous real supply of mortgage credit that is not sensitive to interest rates, and

C = The real cost of capital which is also exogenous.

For simplicity we assume that C is constant, and that the supply of mortgage credit is made up of two components – a non-interest sensitive portion, M^S, and an interest sensitive portion, $e(i_H - C)$. The sensitivity of the latter share is measured by e. Figure 5.1 will help demonstrate how the mortgage market equilibrium can be embedded into the model.

The northeast quadrant depicts the housing market and the axes measure the prices and quantity of housing; the southwest quadrant the mortgage market and the axes measure the mortgage rate and the quantity of mortgage credit; the other two quadrants help show how conditions in the latter market affect those in the former. In the southeast quadrant the schedule corresponds to a transactions demand for money function. It implies that there is a positive relationship between the size of the housing stock HS and the demand for mortgage credit. The schedule in the northwest quadrant indicates that i_H and P_H are negatively related for a given R. Schedule SM^S, in the southwest quadrant, is the mortgage supply function; its shape and location depend upon the proportion of mortgage funds that is not interest sensitive, M^S, and the ease with which funds flow to the mortgage market from other investments when i_H increases relative to C. As the coefficient e increases, SM^S becomes flatter, that is, $S'M^S$ and credit flows more freely between markets.

By shifting the demand for mortgage credit curve along SM^S from DD to $D'D'$ we can derive a mortgage market equilibrium schedule MM in the housing market. Furthermore, by increasing e so that SM^S shifts to $S'M^S$ we can get some notion of how, say, reform of financial institutions might affect the housing market. Curve $M'M'$ in the northwest quadrant is derived from $S'M^S$. The increased flatness of the $M'M'$ curve indicates that reducing credit market segmentation (that is, increasing e) reduces the impact of mortgage market conditions on the housing market.

This can be seen more clearly by focusing on the northeast quadrant of Figure 5.1.

In Figure 5.2 we depict the left hand side of equation (5.1), curve EE, and the assumed fixed stock of housing, HS, the vertical line.

Any given shift in the housing demand curve EE along $M'M'$ produces a smaller increase in i_H. Because e is larger, funds are more responsive, and more funds will flow to the mortgage market for a given change in i_H. The increase in i_H means that equilibrium can be restored to the mortgage only by a decrease in P_H. But, this decrease increases M^S, so that the MM curve shifts to the right. Accordingly, for smaller changes in i_H there are smaller expansionary shifts of the MM curve. Equilibrium will finally be restored at a price higher than the initial price P_I and lower than the initial in-

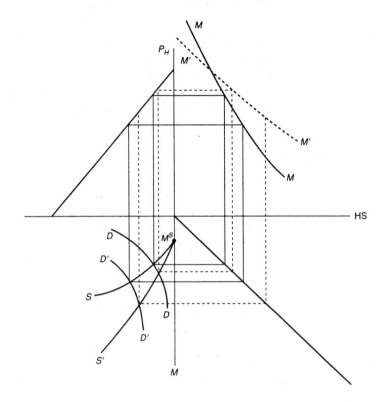

Figure 5.1 Mortgage system – housing-market links

crease to P_S as adjustment in P_H shift the MM curve up and the $E'E'$ curve down.

Taking some comparative statics will help illustrate the workings of the model. Initially we assume that the responsiveness of funds to changes in the mortgage rate is close to zero so that SM^S and MM are relatively steep. When equation (5.2) is solved for i_H we get

$$i_H = [Z_0 + Z_1 Y(1 - t) + Z_2(HH - CH) + Z_4 P_H$$
$$- M^S + eC]/Z_3 + e) \tag{5.3}$$

Substituting equation (5.3) into equation (5.1) and solving for P_H yields:[3]

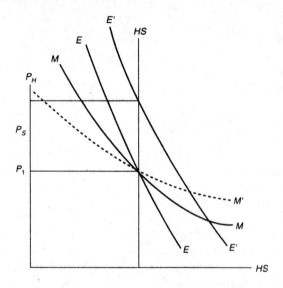

Figure 5.2 Mortgage system – housing-market links

$$P_H = a_0 + a_1 Y(1 - t) + a_2(HH - CH) - a_4 HS$$
$$+ a_3 \Theta t - a_3(Z_0 + Z_1 Y(1 - t) + Z_2(HH - CH)$$
$$+ eC - M^S)/(Z_3 + e]D^1 \qquad (5.4)$$

where $D = 1 + a_3 Z_4/(Z_3 + e)$ and $a_i = B_i/B_4$

From which we get these comparative statics:

$$\frac{dP_H}{d\Theta^3} = a_3 t \ > 0 \qquad (5.5a)$$

$$\frac{dP_H}{dt} = a_3 \Theta + Y(a_3 Z_1)/(Z_3 + e)\ D \qquad (5.5b)$$

$$\frac{dP_H}{dY} = (1 - t)(a_1 - a_3 Z_1)/(Z_3 + e)\ D \qquad (5.5c)$$

$$\frac{dP_H}{dM^s} = a_3/(Z_3 + e)D \tag{5.5d}$$

$$\frac{dP_H}{dHH} = (a_2 - a_3Z_2)/(Z_3 + e)D \tag{5.5e}$$

$$\frac{dP_H}{dCH} = (a_3Z_2 - a_2)/(Z_3 + e)D \tag{5.5f}$$

Outside of (5.5a) and (5.5d), the comparative statics of equation (5.5) cannot be signed without specific assumptions about the elasticities of the variables, or without the assumption that the mortgage market is supply-constrained.[4] In some respects, this result may be somewhat unsatisfactory: more restrictions are needed in order to predict how the variables will interact, but from a policy perspective the opposite is true. For instance, in order to argue that an increase in public-housing production will have a negative effect on the demand for owner-occupied housing, assumptions about the interest rate and demographic elasticities of demand must be explicit. The clarification of assumptions that are in fact implicit in a policy measure should help to improve the understanding of the policies undertaken.

Furthermore, if we consider the implications of a movement away from the static equilibrium described by equations (5.5), we find signs of the impact elasticities to be less important: they can change depending upon the steady-state growth rate. For example, equation (5.5b) is ambiguous, even though Hadjimatheou's work (1976) suggests that it is positive for the UK. As Mayes (1979) points out, however, Hadjimatheou's analysis neglects the income effect – the second term in (5.5b). If $dP_H/dY > 0$, then the sign of (5.5b) depends upon the substitution effect being larger than the income effect. Because the size of the substitution effect is a function of the inflation rate, so too is the sign of (5.5b). Hence, not only are the quantitative impacts of various policies affected by the anticipated rate of inflation, the qualitative effects are also.

If policy-makers are constrained to considering the impact of changes in such observable market indicators as the level of the mortgage rate, and if the qualitative impact of these variables can change for different Θs, then policy is indeed bounded by a large margin of error and may easily be perverse. An increase in the mortgage rate, for example, may correspond to an increase or a decrease in the real cost of borrowing. For empirical work the solution to this problem is careful specification along the lines used by Davidson *et al.* (1978). In addition, a stylized version of their approach can help yield some insights into the effects of various policies when the instruments used to affect policy are in nominal terms, and when there is uncertainty about Θ so that one knows only that Θ has changed, but not by how much.

For example, consider changes in the nominal mortgage rate. As explained earlier, in order for increases in the nominal rate to decrease the demand for housing, the increase must exceed the increase in the anticipated rate of inflation by some multiple of Θ. If one assumes that an increase in the inflation rate causes the nominal mortgage rate to increase by Θ, and that the sign of the impact coefficient for the nominal mortgage rate is nevertheless less than zero, then because the relative return to home-ownership rises with Θ – tending to offset the negative effects of an inflation-caused increase in the mortgage rate – it is not unreasonable to suppose that the negative impact is weaker at higher levels of inflation.[5] To account for this we can substitute the nominal mortgage rate for i_H, and $a'3/\Theta$ for $a3$ and rewrite equation (5.4) as:

$$P_H = a_0 + a_1 Y(1 - t) + a_2(HH - CH) - a_4 HS$$
$$- a'_3/\Theta(Z + e)[Z_0 + Z_1 Y(1 - t) + Z_2(HH - CH)$$
$$- M^S + eC]D \qquad (5.6)$$

The following partials can be derived from equation (5.6).

$$\frac{dP_H}{d\Theta} = a'_3 i_H/[\Theta(Z_3 + e)D]^2 \qquad (5.7a)$$

$$\frac{dP_H}{dt} = (Z_1 a'_3/(Z_3 + e)D^\Theta - a_1) \qquad (5.7b)$$

$$\frac{dP_H}{dY} = (1 - t)(a_1 - Z_1 a'_3/(Z_3 + e)D^\Theta) \qquad (5.7c)$$

$$\frac{dP_H}{dM^s} = a'_3/\Theta(Z_3 + e)D > 0 \tag{5.7d}$$

$$\frac{dP_H}{dHH} = (a_2 - a'_3 Z_2)/(Z_3 + e)\Theta\, D \tag{5.7e}$$

$$\frac{dP_H}{dCH} = (a'_3 Z_2)/(Z_3 + e)\Theta\, D - a_2 \tag{5.7f}$$

To examine the 'theory' suggested by these derivatives, and those in (5.5), it is helpful to consider some policy issues, such as those discussed in Chapter 2.

5.2 POLICY ANALYSIS IN THE MODEL

Anticipated Inflation, Taxes and the Demand for Housing

Equations (5.5a) and (5.7a) imply that, in the short-run at least, the relative price of housing is positively related to the anticipated rate of inflation. Because of the nominal basis of the income tax, or deposit-rate ceilings, the real after-tax rate of return on all taxed assets declines with inflation-related increases in nominal yield. For most households in developing countries home-ownership presents the only virtually tax-free investment option, and declining yields elsewhere will bid up the valuation of home-ownership. The implicit tax subsidy becomes more valuable as the inflation rate increases. The impact on house prices of changes in Θ is, in large part, determined by the interest rate sensitivity of housing demand, a_3 and a_3'; the higher the sensitivity the greater the impact.

These equations also suggest that the impact of the income tax rate cannot be determined *a priori*. The sign of the income effect in (5.5b) is determined by the sign of (5.5c). And while in the model (5.5c) cannot be signed, there is empirical work for developed countries (by Byatt, Holmans and Laidler, 1973; and by Wilkinson, 1973) that indicates that (5.5c) is greater than zero, so that the income effect of a tax increase in (5.5b) is negative and offsets, at least to some extent, the positive substitution effect.

The empirical finding that the demand for housing is a positive function of income is not surprising in terms of the model, which says that the sign of (5.5c) depends upon the income and interest-rate elasticities of the demand for housing and mortgage credit. One would expect the income elasticity of the demand for housing to exceed the income elasticity of the demand for mortgage credit for a number of reasons.[6] But the interest-rate elasticities need not have the same relation. The interest-rate elasticity of the demand for housing is reduced by the transaction costs of moving house, whereas the interest-rate elasticity of the demand for mortgage credit is not. Even if the latter does not exceed the former, (5.5c) is positive if the income elasticity of the demand for housing exceeds that of the demand for mortgage credit by a greater amount than a_3 exceeds Z_3.

Comparing (5.7c) and (5.5c), that is, our static and steady-state views, we find that in the latter the income elasticity of the demand for housing is a function of the inflation-related tax subsidy for home-ownership. This result is not surprising inasmuch as imputed rent can be viewed as a form of income and this rent increases with increases in Θ. As a result, the higher is Θ, the more real income measures that do not include imputed rent understate real purchasing power. This finding points to the possible dangers of using cross-sectional estimates of income elasticity for planning or forecasting purposes. It also suggests another explanation for finding different measures of income elasticity for housing in the same country in different years, as Wilkinson (1973) finds for the UK, and Malpezzi and Mayo (1987a) show for a number of countries.

Anticipated inflation also affects the impact of public-housing production and household formation (5.7e) and (5.7f) on the housing market. If (Z_3) is positive, as empirical work suggests, then it increases the impact of both factors. With respect to household formation the results are in accordance with common sense. If the return to home-ownership is higher for a higher inflation rate, more households will select that tenure. The larger negative impact of public-housing production for a higher rate of inflation requires some explanation. First, consider equation (5.5f). The reduced demand for home-ownership associated with a higher level of construction of public units decreases the demand for mortgage credit. This reduction in demand for credit partially offsets the direct effect of public-unit production. Equation (5.7f) differs from (5.5f) in that a higher rate of inflation reduces the amount by which this offsetting credit side-effect reduces the real side impact. Hence, the direct impact is larger.

The Mortgage Market

Following the sharp house price increases of the early 1970s and the late 1980s in a number of developed economies, *inter alia*, the US, the UK, Finland, Japan, and Sweden, there was considerable attention given to the role of mortgage lending as a catalyst for house price increases. Implicit in this concern was the view that mortgage lending helped fuel speculative bubbles. Although the effect on the housing market of mortgage lending is ultimately an empirical question, the model can help sort our some of the assumptions implicit in the argument.

Both equations (5.5d) and (5.7d) suggest that house prices are a positive function of the supply of mortgage credit. In both equations the size of the impact is directly related to the interest-rate sensitivity of home buyers and inversely related to the interest-rate sensitivity of mortgagors. One possible interpretation of the argument that lending practices have no impact on house prices is to say that e approaches infinity, so that the cost of capital for housing is completely described in equation (5.1). In this case consideration of the mortgage market equilibrium, that is equation (5.2), becomes unnecessary. One could also argue that if there is some degree of segmentation in the capital markets, then credit mortgage credit policies can influence house prices.

Finally, equation (5.7d) points out that the higher the Θ, the weaker are restrictions on lending as a means to reduce house price increases.

Selected Policies

Other policies are also amenable to analysis within this type of model. To mention a few:

1. It is possible, for example, to examine the status of first-time home-buyers. Looking at equation (5.5), one sees that besides addressing social equity concerns, such a policy also contributes to housing market stability. Efforts by governments to place a

higher priority on loan applications from first-time buyers, as is the case in Hungary, tend to increase Z_2 – by improving the access of new households to the mortgage market – relative to B_2 and thereby reduce the impact on house price, of changes in household formation and or government housing production. By increasing Z_2 this policy causes the demand curve for mortgage credit to shift out by a greater amount for a given increase in households. Like financial reform measures which cause e to increase, e, this policy causes the $M'M'$ curve in the northeast quadrant to be flatter. As we showed earlier, this flattening out of the MM curve implies that an increase in household formation (or a decrease in public-housing production) corresponds to a smaller increase in the mortgage rate. New households are, in effect, able to 'crowd-out' current home-owners from the credit markets, and thereby reduce the pressures on the housing market of the short-run adjustments to changes in household formation and/or government production of council units.

2. In a number of countries research efforts are examining how to establish a more stable, broader-based supply of mortgage credit. Equation (5.2) can help clarify this issue. The more segmented the mortgage market is from other financial markets, the steeper is the mortgage market counterpart to the LM curve. If government policy could make mortgage investment more like other investments so the e is larger, the model implies that housing production would be less sensitive to financial flows, but more sensitive to changes in the demand for housing. In the limit, making e infinite would eliminate the need to consider the mortgage market; i_H in equation (5.1) would yield all the information needed.

3. In conjunction with the previous issue, one might want to look at how the sale of publically-owned houses would affect the mortgage rate under various financial regimes. The impact of any program of public housing-unit sales obviously depends upon its operational structure and constraints. But to take an illustrative example, suppose such a program increases the supply and demand for housing units by the same amount, so that there is no direct impact on the housing market. Suppose further that such a program increases the demand for mortgage credit through an increase in Z_0. Differentiating equation (5.3) we find that

$di_H/dZ_0 = 1/(e + Z_3) > 0$. This result implies that: (1) the sale of public housing will increase other home-owner's mortgage rates for $e \neq \infty$. Simply put, more households demand mortgage credit. And while this change represents little other than a change in the title of the debtors from local governments to households, imperfections in the mortgage market imply that (1) the supply of mortgage credit will increase only if the interest rate rises; and (2) the impact is inversely related to the interest-rate elasticity of demand of mortgage credit. The lower the sensitivity of home-buyers to interest-rate changes, the greater the rate increase required to equilibrate the market.

5.3 CONCLUSION

Because of the unobservable prices and subsidies that affect housing and tenure choice decisions, and the way these 'off the book' factors can be affected by the inflation rate, care must be taken in constructing the explanations that underlie both our views and our empirical studies of the housing sector. The model presented here is one way of sorting out some of the important relationships that affect the housing sector. It is worth stressing, however, that it is not the particular relationships specified that are ultimately of importance. Rather, it is the demonstration of the relevance of a thoroughly developed, yet fairly simple paradigm for housing-sector analysis. Depending upon the question at hand, housing researchers and policy advisors should be able to use this approach to 'roll their own' models.

Part II

Case Studies

6 The Financial Dimension: Mortgage Instruments

6.1 INTRODUCTION

The failings of mortgage systems indexed to purchasing power in Argentina, Brazil, Chile, and Paraguay have made economists' claims that mortgage indexation would be an effective way of making housing more affordable while simultaneously fighting inflation, appear naive.[1] During the debt crisis two of these countries introduced policies of deindexation of prices. Chile closed down its mortgage lenders in the late 1970s, and Paraguay abandoned indexed mortgage finance in 1982.[2]

It is now fairly clear that designing a mortgage finance system that can deal with both inflationary and real-side shocks is much like fighting a many-headed monster. This is the case because of the interrelations between the different aspects of housing finance, particularly the countervailing forces of sustainability of funds for the lending institutions and affordability of funds for the borrower. For example, lowering the initial costs of financing so that home-ownership becomes more affordable can make the system unsustainable; the real rate of return can become so low that the supply of funds mobilized to fund such 'affordable' mortgages continually contracts in real terms. In this case, dealing with the affordability problem simply makes the funding-sustainability problem worse.

Similarly, increasing future mortgage repayment to match increases in inflation, preserves the real value of funds that are mobilized. But, unless the income of borrowers enables them to keep pace with the increases in prices, payments can become unaffordable. That is, when mortgages are tied to a price index, households cannot always continue to make the repayments promptly, particularly if real income suddenly falls sharply.

The difficulty in instrument design is that solving an inflation-related contracting problem seems to create another problem in its

73

stead. It is not surprising, therefore, that the record of mortgage finance systems in developing countries experiencing high rates of inflation, is not a happy one. Besides the failed systems in Argentina, Brazil, and Chile, a number of other countries – the Philippines, Ecuador, and until the late 1980s, Mexico and Turkey – have either virtually stopped all mortgage lending, or resorted to large government transfers to sustain the supply of mortgage credit when inflation increased.[3] In short, it appears that more often than not, the monster has won. As we will discuss, sometimes by design and sometimes in execution, the systems introduced have often been faulty.

The purpose of this chapter is to show that when carefully considered, it is possible in most cases to balance the need for an affordable and sustainable means of housing finance by introducing a mortgage contract that addresses the concerns implied by the macroeconomic situation. Instruments can be designed which keep pace with borrowers' ability to repay while not ignoring lenders' concerns. For example, by allowing loan maturity to vary, an instrument can be constructed that reconciles any difference in loan value implied by satisfying the different parties' concerns. Such instruments effectively provide for the possibility of the rescheduling, rather than the forgiving of real payments. Further, they can be designed to provide this kind of assistance if, and only if, it is needed. Variants of this approach were recently introduced in Mexico, Ghana, Poland, Turkey and Hungary (see Maydon *et al.*, 1988), and in many circumstances, as pointed out by Lessard and Modigliani (1975), such instruments can be highly beneficial to the economy and the financial system.

This chapter demonstrates the advantages of one of these instruments, the dual-indexed mortgage, by examining a series of conjectural interactions between inflation and wage behavior. It considers a number of 'what if' kinds of questions about how such an instrument would work if various wage, cost, and inflationary conditions were to prevail in the economy. By how much, for instance, would loan repayment be affected by rising inflation, falling wages and high construction costs? It allows policy-makers to consider how variations in loan terms, housing standards and rates of return will affect return and sustainability. In short, the model permits analysts to create anticipated environments and then examine how varying loan terms will affect the viability of the contract.

In brief, then, this chapter identifies the important questions that need to be addressed in designing mortgage instruments under conditions of high and variable inflation and fluctuating real wages. In carrying out this analysis some simulations of how the model applies to the Turkish historical experience are made.

Section 6.2 discusses the affordability problem of financing housing in an inflationary setting. Section 6.3 first discusses the shortcomings of credit subsidies as a means to offset the affordability problem. This is followed by a discussion of indexation as an alternative to credit subsidies. Here, the pitfalls of various indexation schemes are addressed – especially the failure of various schemes to consider the effects real wage reductions would have on the ability of borrowers to repay loans. Section 6.4 shows how a system of dual indexation would compare with single index instruments. It also deals with administrative issues of dual indexed mortgages, such as the importance of matching unit size with households income. The last section concludes.

6.2 THE REPAYMENT 'TILT': HOW INFLATION MAKES HOUSING UNAFFORDABLE

In discussing the affordability of mortgage finance, it is helpful to distinguish between two kinds of affordability problems. The first one is faced by those whose resources are so low that they cannot afford the minimum standard of shelter that is available. Their problems are most effectively addressed by improvements in the functioning of basic infrastructure supply and/or providing tenure security. The encouragement of home-ownership through a more efficient housing finance system is not the most practical direct method of providing shelter for the poor. Perhaps the central lesson of the shelter projects in developing countries is that, in a physical design sense, housing can be made affordable to most households (see World Bank, 1980).

The second type of affordability problem arises because when contracts are written in nominal terms, inflation makes housing unaffordable to most families at market rates of interest. The focus here is on mortgage contracting procedures that can address this latter housing-affordability problem. From this perspective, the objective for redesigning mortgage contracts is to eliminate the financial constraints that impede the affordability of housing for greater numbers of lower-and moderate-income households. The objectives are not to produce more housing, although that outcome will often result. Rather, it is to provide a financing vehicle so that those who can afford to, and so desire, can purchase homes.

During 1934–59, lenders throughout the world relied largely on fixed-rate, equal-payment mortgages.[4] With these instruments, even if real interest rates remain low, expectations of increasing inflation can raise the nominal interest rates on long-term mortgage debt very quickly. Even with mild inflation loan-affordability will be significantly reduced because although there may not be a change in the real interest rate, such mortgages 'redistribute' real payments toward the early years of the loan.[5] This tilting of the real repayment stream causes an increasing mismatch between real loan repayments and the income capacity of households over the life of the loan.

Consider, for example, a household with a family income of $3 000 per year, and paying 20 percent of this initial income for mortgage payments on a 30-year fully amortizing fixed-rate loan. In a world of zero inflation, and 3 percent real interest rate, this payment would be sufficient to finance a loan for almost $12 000, an amount four times the annual income. If inflation increases to 10 percent, nominal lending rates rise to approximately 13 percent to compensate the lender for the erosion in the value of later payments. With the same share of income the household can now afford a mortgage of only $4 500, a figure 1.5 times more than annual income. Put another way, when the inflation rate increases by 10 percent, households must more than double the initial share of income spent on mortgage repayments in order to finance the same amount of real debt. At the same time, however, the real payments required in the latter years of the loan are cut in half.

Given the scale of the increase in payment burden that occurs with only a 10 percent increase in the rate of inflation – a rate less than one-fifth the rate experienced by developing countries over 1983–7 – it is obvious that in developing countries, mortgage credit is not affordable for most families.[6]

6.3 ADDRESSING THE REPAYMENT TILT PROBLEM

Until the early 1980s, the mortgage repayment tilt problem was treated in one of two ways: first, as an affordability problem that required subsidies; or second, as a contracting problem that could be solved by redesigning the mortgage instrument. In principle, this second approach attempts to deal with the concern of lenders by ensuring that the real value of repayments is not affected by inflation. It is discussed more fully later. But, first consider the first approach – credit subsidies – as a means of addressing the inflation-caused affordability problems.

Credit Subsidies as a Response to High Interest Rates

Most countries in the world have at one time or another used interest-rate subsidies to reduce mortgage borrowing costs. With this approach cash flow problems are solved by 'retilting' the early payments back to what they would have been without inflation. Credit subsidies are used to 'buy down' the cost of housing finance with below-market interest rates. While this practice is widespread, there are four problems with it.

First, if the objective of the subsidy is to increase housing consumption, then, because credit is at least partially fungible, subsidizing credit is less efficient than is subsidizing the housing expenditure. It is inefficient because, as Meltzer (1974) shows, over the long term such a subsidy permits households to substitute credit for their own savings and, thereby, free their savings to be used for other purchases. Hence, it allows the subsidies to be spent on activities other than those it was intended to encourage. Consequently, the efficiency of the subsidy in inducing the intended behavior is diminished.

Second, below-market credit provides a subsidy to solve what is most cases is a contracting problem. At rates of inflation lower than 25–30 percent a year, carefully designed mortgage-indexation schemes can eliminate the cash-flow costs imposed by high nominal payments, and do so without subsidy.[7] While it is difficult to measure precisely how much a credit subsidy really is, because of the difficulties in projecting inflation and the appropriate real interest rate, the per-unit subsidy level necessary to eliminate the inflation-relating tilting of repayment is clearly very large. For instance, with an inflation

Case Studies

Table 6.1   Credit subsidies implied by different interest terms

Expected inflation rate (percentage)	Real interest rate (percentage)	Subsidy rate needed to eliminate tilt (percentage)
15	8	53
30	8	71
30	10	68
40	8	77
30	6	73

rate of 30 percent and a real interest rate of 8 percent, the subsidy necessary to eliminate the tilt problem for a middle-income borrower is in the order of 70 percent.

In Table 6.1 the implied subsidy rate is given for a 15-year mortgage with various assumptions about real interest rates, expected inflation, and the nominal interest rate charged. The last column shows the subsidy rate required to get mortgage payments back to the same proportion of family income put towards payments when there is no inflation.

Third, interest rate subsidies do not really solve the repayment tilt problem by reducing the higher costs in the early years of a loan. Instead, they reduce real repayments throughout the loan's life. As a result, with a subsidy, interest payments in the later years of the loan can become trivial rather than just small. For example, instead of being required to allocate as much as 60 percent of income to repayments, as could be the case with a fixed-rate loan, a subsidy sufficient to reduce early payments to affordable levels would call for repayments in later years that account for 1 percent or 2 percent of income. This kind of subsidy mechanism gives beneficiaries larger than necessary subsidies.

The final problem with credit subsidies is that the aggregate level of subsidy needed to eliminate the effects of inflation on housing affordability is simply too large. For example, Figure 6.1 shows the income group for which fixed nominal-payment mortgage instruments become unaffordable due to an increase in the rate of inflation.

The income distribution figures are for urban family income in Turkey, 1985.[8] Point *A* represents the income level needed for buying a house that costs 2.5 times the median urban family income, if the household was able to make a 30 percent down payment and could finance a 20-year fixed interest-rate loan with 25 percent of their income. Interest on the loan at 15 percent reflects a 6 percent real interest rate and the slightly less than 9 percent inflation rate that characterized 1950–74 in Turkey. The income needed to qualify is slightly more than the median income level, the 60th percentile.

Point *B*, the ninetieth percentile, reflects the income level needed to finance a fixed interest-rate loan that incorporates the higher inflation rates of more recent years. Instead of a 15 percent nominal interest rate, the appropriate nominal interest rate is 38 percent. The increase in inflation from 9 percent to approximately 30 percent per year has, in the absence of contracts that adjust for the change in the distribution of real repayments, priced home-ownership beyond the ability to pay for most families. Hence, the absence of indexed mortgage contracts priced all those between the sixtieth and ninetieth percentiles out of the housing market. If these households require the level of subsidy for a 30 percent rate of inflation described in Table 6.1, about 70 percent, the scale of the government expenditures needed to eliminate the tilt problem for all the families affected would be enormous and not sustainable.

Indexed Mortgage: Indexed to Wage or Price?

The central problem facing housing-finance institutions in an inflationary environment is sustaining the flow of funds. Indexed mortgage contracts seem to be a promising way to deal with this problem. For lenders, they preserve the real value of the repayments over the maturity of the loan. For borrowers, if indexation reduces the large payment burden in the early years of repayment, they may help prevent them from being locked out of the housing market by a cash-flow constraint. Yet, as suggested earlier, recent experience with indexed mortgage contracts in a number of countries has underscored the point that indexation to prices or wages is not by any means an automatic solution to housing-finance problems. In order to consider the types of problems that can arise, it is helpful to consider a hypothetical example in a real historical setting.

Consider the situation of a middle-income Turkish family in 1987 earning 733 000 Turkish Lira (TL), approximately US$500, per month who wants to construct and purchase a 70-square meter home.[9] Assume

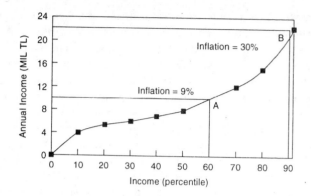

Figure 6.1 Share of Turkish urban households able to afford mortgage repayments with different rates of inflation

first that the house costs 230 000 TL per square meter to build for a total cost of 16 100 000 TL; second, assume a loan is provided at a 75 percent loan-to-value ratio so that the family can borrow 12 075 000 TL; third, inflation is running at 30 percent annually; fourth, the rate of interest charged the family is the market rate of 38 percent (that implies a real interest rate of approximately 6 percent; fifth, during an 18-month construction period, no payments are made but interest is capitalized at 38 percent; and sixth, once completed, the family begins to amortize the loan, which has a beginning balance of almost 16 000 000 TL).

Now, consider how the family's earnings are likely to behave. Assume the future income of the family follows the same general pattern of real wage behavior that has occurred in the past. For the examples that follows, actual historical wage data for 1966–86 were used in reverse chronological order. That is, because the economy in Turkey has recently been more turbulent, it was assumed that the initial future years would most likely mirror the recent past, and that in more remote future years conditions would revert to what they have been throughout most of Turkey's history.

The data come from the wage indices for Turkish civil servants, one of the more volatile indices and, therefore, a conservative choice to demonstrate the effects of indexation.[10] The data series for recent years are shown in Figure 6.2.

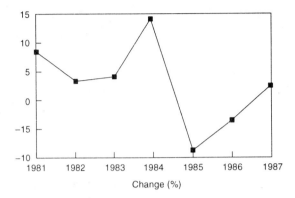

Figure 6.2   Turkey: civil servant salaries (annual percentage change – TI/day)

With fixed nominal annual payments, 6 069 000 TL would be required to amortize the loan over a 20-year period. This is a large amount even for this moderate to upper-income household. In order for such a loan to be amortized payments would have to account for almost 70 percent of the family income in the early years of the loan before dwindling to under 10 percent in later years. Clearly few families would enter into such contracts.

One way to lower the high front-end costs is to index the monthly mortgage payments to the overall increases in prices in the economy. Thus, if the lender required the payment level to increase 30 percent each year to keep pace with inflation, the real value of the payment stream would not be eroded by inflation. The real payment stream would become identical to the nominal payment stream under conditions of no inflation. This is shown in Figure 6.3. Indexation shifts area *ABC* in the figure to the figure to the later years of the loan. As discussed earlier, however, such a solution leaves unchecked the vulnerability of the borrower to wage shocks.

For example, if payments start at 25 percent of income and were allowed to rise along with the price level at 30 percent each year while real wages followed the historical pattern, a repeat of the Turkish past would result in significant increases in the share of income devoted to repayments. The overall pattern is not terribly disruptive, with the percentage of income allocated to payments rising

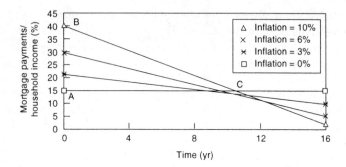

Figure 6.3   Mortgage payments for a house under different inflation
rates

to just over 33 percent at its highest point. It is worth remembering,
however, that this increase in the share of income allocated to mortgage
repayments would come at the same time that real income would
be declining. As a result, there would be an inherent difficulty with
this form of indexation. Depending on the behavior of real wages,
the income percentages allocated to payments could be much higher,
and increase at exactly the 'wrong' times. It is this kind of problem
that has created serious drawbacks for payments in Brazil and
Argentina.[11]

In short, mortgages that rely on price indexes can experience problems when the level of the borrowers' income does not keep pace
with the general level of prices in the economy. When the burden
of real mortgage repayments increases, repayment becomes more
uncertain. When this happens, the lending institution is faced with
the prospect of large numbers of defaults on its loans. When real
wages oscillate, the indexation of repayments to prices does not
eliminate the tilt in the repayment stream in Figure 6.3. Instead it
replaces the initial tilt of the real payment/income ratio with the
possibility of 'hills' and 'valleys' in the ratio. Real payments are
constant, but real income is not. Hence, there remains the possibility of sharp increases in the payment burden ratio.

Attempts to address this hills and valleys problem in the payment-to-income ratio have prompted some countries to focus their
indexation schemes on wage, rather than price, indices. Typically, a
fixed proportion of family income – for example, 25 percent – is

designated for repayment of the mortgage. Each year, as wages nominally increase, so do the monthly payments. The advantage of this approach is that it protects borrowers from the sudden shocks that can occur if real incomes fall, since the portion of income devoted to repayment remains the same.

Using the same Turkish wage data and capping monthly payments at 25 percent of income, we find that real payments are sometimes higher and sometimes lower than those in the price indexation system. But, because of the cap on the amount of increase, real wage reductions would not require increases in the share of income allocated to repayments. Similarly, because payments increase with wage increases, the reduction in the ratio due to increasing wages would also be eliminated. In the end, however, all is not sanguine with this method of indexation. While borrowers are protected under a system of wage indexation, the lender would not be afforded the same protection.

Lenders' protection would be reduced, because if wages fall, the amount that would have been required to preserve the real value of the payment and to match inflation is implicitly 'forgiven'. For the lender not to incur a loss, he must realize real-payment increases of sufficient size and timing to offset the losses. Depending upon the pattern of the amounts 'forgiven', they can amount to a substantial subsidy on the part of the lender. In the Turkish example, the present value of this subsidy would amount to some 20 percent.

So far, two forms of indexation – one tying payments to prices, the other tying payments to wages – have been shown to be flawed, if and when real wages fall. On the one hand, indexing payments to inflation places the risk on the shoulders of the borrower, whose concern is that payments can quickly become unaffordable when real wages do not keep pace with inflation. On the other hand, indexing payments to wages places the onus on the lender. The lender must take the risk that real wages will be unaffected by inflation. If they are not, the lender may recoup only a portion of the real amount lent.

Combining Wage and Price Indices

One way out of this quandary was recently introduced in new regulations for the Mass Housing Fund in Turkey, and the Central Banks in Mexico and Ghana.[12] This method involves a dual system of wage and price indexation designed to tackle the concerns of both borrowers and lenders. Borrower concerns are addressed – loan repayments are indexed to wages, so that a borrower never has to pay a portion of his income that exceeds a comfortable or commonly accepted level (about 25 percent). At the same time, lenders' concerns are taken care of because, first, the loan balance is indexed to prices rather than wages, so that any portion of interest and principal due over and above a given portion of income is capitalized into the amount of the loan outstanding. Second, the loan maturity is variable to permit shortfalls in real repayments to be offset, or earlier real repayments to pay off the loan more rapidly.

Like instruments that rely on a wage index, with a dual-index instrument real repayments are accelerated in years when incomes are rising relative to inflation, and repaid more slowly in years when real wages fall. Unlike a wage-indexed loan, however, the real value of the loan is no longer uncertain. In principle, with this instrument it is the loan's maturity date rather than its value that is uncertain. In practice, the analytical question becomes one of setting an initial loan-maturity schedule, such that the loan terms provide for a sufficient amount of possible maturity extension, so that any shortfalls in real payments can be accommodated by term lengthening.

For example, loan terms could be set so that in the absence of any real wage changes the loan would fully amortize in 15 years. But borrowers could be told that a payment of a specific percent of their income for 20 years assures full repayment of the loan. In this case lenders gain the possibility of five more years of repayments to 'cushion' any losses attributable to payment reductions due to real wage declines not offsetting payment increases.[13] The cost to borrowers of this kind of arrangement is that the payments are initially higher because the original loan is set to amortize in 15 rather than 20 years. Borrowers, however, also gain from this method of indexation because real wage increases amortize the loan more rapidly, and accordingly, their loan can be paid off earlier if such gains are achieved. With systems that relied only upon wage indexation, the value of these accelerated repayments did not accrue to borrowers. Most importantly, borrowers gain from this method of financing because the lender or the government bears the risk that even with maturity lengthening, the loan may not amortize. In a sense, this arrangement is much like writing an insurance contract with deductibles: borrowers are responsible for anticipated possible volatility in real wages, but they are not responsible beyond some limit.

In summary, a dual-index mortgage is like wage indexation in its attempts to balance out fluctuations in real repayments over the course of the loan. Unlike wage indexation, however, balance is achieved not only by smoothing the hills and valleys of the payment-to-income payment ratio, but also by allowing the length of the repayment period to vary. In other words, the constancy of the ratio is maintained by building-in what we have termed a rescheduling cushion of sufficient length, so that the loan is fully repaid.

It is, of course, possible that if the real wage environment is sufficiently volatile, the size of the rescheduling cushion needed to amortize the loan may become so large – even infinite – that the initial payments are not reduced very much relative to what they would be with a nominal interest-rate loan. Alternatively, loan forgiveness may be necessary at the end of the loan. Even in the relatively volatile Turkish wage environment, however, a five-year rescheduling cushion would have been sufficient for full repayment, as long as the initial housing standards matched the household's initial income level. As the next section suggests the model can be useful in the important issue of the sorting of housing standard and initial income levels.

6.4 ADMINISTERING DUAL-INDEXED MORTGAGES: HOW A MODEL CAN HELP

A mortgage is affordable to a borrower when the borrower's payment of a reasonable percentage of income over a fairly long period of time fully amortizes the loan. This definition generally incorporates the expectation that, although economic conditions may vary considerably, they will not become, and remain unduly harsh for extended periods of time. If they do, no financial instrument will work. For example, while the Turkish real wage reductions in recent years were often precipitous, they have not been lasting. Indeed, they have been accompanied by sharp increases in real *per capita* income.

One difference between a world of relatively low inflation, steady real wage growth, and fixed-rate mortgages (that is, pre-1975), and a world of high and variable inflation, real wage shocks and indexed mortgages (that is, the present), is that affordability is much harder to calculate in the current environment. Determining the maximum amount that a household can afford to borrow is a straightforward calculation if the loan is a fixed-rate, fixed-term mortgage. Once the maximum mortgage amount is known, calculating whether or not a unit is affordable is not very difficult. When inflation increases it may be close to impossible for most families to afford to pay off such loans, but it is not difficult to calculate this lack of affordability. By contrast, in an era of inflation and wage uncertainty, determining the maximum affordable loan, and therefore the housing unit size, is less easy because the value of repayments is contingent upon so many hard-to-predict factors. This is why simple models of mortgage repayment can be useful.

Table 6.2 shows how, by charting different trends in the factors affecting repayment, such models can help estimate the appropriate unit size or loan amount for different income classes. For instance, as indicated by the table, one of the most important factors driving affordability for a household, is the real interest rate. If all other factors are held constant, except this real rate, the size of the unit affordable for a household in a given income class can vary by up to 20 square meters, and the gap is much greater across income levels.

Alternatively, an economy that is experiencing more severe volatility would require a longer period of possible rescheduling, and correspondingly, a shorter maturity for the loan to amortize if no wage reductions occur. Such models can help trace through the effects of real wage volatility on the size of unit that is affordable for a given income level.

Similarly, such models could be used to translate the effects of greater real wage uncertainty on the length of the rescheduling cushion and/or subsidy that would be needed to provide the financing for a housing unit of a particular size. In short, under conditions of inflation and real wage volatility, such modeling exercises are essential for policy-makers, lenders, and borrowers to make better informed judgments about whether or not an indexed mortgage scheme is workable in a particular economic environment.

Early experience with dual-indexed loans suggests that because the dual-indexed mechanism is so different from traditional ones that in some countries a shift to such an instrument will require a

Table 6.2 Affordable house sizes in square meters for various
construction periods if real wages are constant

	18-month construction period, 25 percent of income			33-month construction period, 25 percent of income		
Family monthly income (TL 1,000s)	260	533	733	260	533	733
Real interest rate						
0.05	40	80	100	30	60	90
0.06	30	70	90	<30	50	70
0.08	30	60	80	<30	40	60

Note: a 75 percent loan-to-value ratio and construction costs of TL 230,000 per square meter. The income levels listed correspond approximately to the 25th, 50th and 75th percentiles of urban household incomes in 1987.

comprehensive reorganization of the repayment collection system. The use of a new software package and reorientation of the staff may be needed so that the underwriting requirements protect both lenders and borrowers. For example, borrowers whose real payments have been accelerated need to be told that their debt is terminated earlier. Even more important, loan terms need to be set so that the rescheduling period does not simply become a means of providing implicit subsidies. While there is no doubt that this system is more administratively complex, there is also no doubt that these higher administrative costs are but a fraction of the costs involved with providing either 'affordable' fixed-interest-rate loans or partially indexed loans. It can often be considerably less risky to use this approach than relying upon only a wage or price index instrument. In addition, if wage indices are politically, rather than economically determined, as is the case in many countries, or these indices are not credible as may be the case in reforming socialist economies, different ways of payment-smoothing may be appropriate.[14]

6.5 CONCLUSION

Mortgage indexation has been tried in a number of countries as an alternative to lowering interest rates through subsidies. Thus far, its effectiveness as a means of making mortgage finance more affordable has been mixed. Its failings, however, have not been the result of the naive application of an abstract economic concept to real world problems. Nor have the failings been the inevitable consequence of surrendering to inflation. Rather, problems have arisen for two reasons.

First, under the extremely high rates of inflation that have occurred, indexation of mortgage repayments provides little help. When inflation rates exceed 50 percent per year, even indexed instruments cannot adjust fast enough to keep up with the inflation rate.[15] Second, there have often been inherent flaws in the way repayments have been implemented. Adequate attention was not paid to the effects that real wage volatility could have on loan values. In some cases, provision was not made for the kind of real wage shocks that occurred, that is, only prices indexes were used. In others, too much provision was allowed, that is, only wage indexes were used.

A dual-indexed mortgage contract in principle provides the kind of cushioning against these shocks that can make housing finance both affordable and in most circumstances sustainable. Moreover, simple models can be used to determine whether this type of instrument can be effectively implemented in a particular economic environment.[16] Nevertheless, the difficulties in implementing this kind of instrument should not be understated. How reliable, for example, are the wage indexes to be used? Are these indexes produced on a timely basis? How will the funding for the risk of continual decline in real payments be structured? Finally, who will ensure that prudential concerns are emphasized in the development of loan terms? For this kind of instrument to work and be sustainable, these kinds of technical questions require equally technical, rather than political, answers. Otherwise, dual-indexed instruments can easily become an even more circuitous way of providing credit subsidies.

7 The Financial Policy Dimension: Competition for Deposits

7.1 INTRODUCTION

The role of monetary balances in economic growth has long been a topic of macroeconomic research; see, among others, Levhari and Patinkin (1968). Following the work of Sinai and Stokes (1972), a number of studies have given this perspective empirical content. By demonstrating the significance of the role of monetary balances in an aggregate production function, this work has shown that money and financial policy need to be carefully considered in studies of growth. More recently this type of empirical analysis has been extended to the production function of a developing country, Pakistan, by Khan and Ahmad (1985). Their results are consistent with the findings for the US and Japan – that is, real money balances are an important factor of production.

This chapter also examines the role of real money balances in an aggregate production function of a developing economy, Colombia. In addition to being a developing country, Colombia is also interesting to analyze in this way for a number of other reasons. First, although it has experienced high and variable rates of inflation, it has also introduced a competitive system of quasi-monetary balances that have been indexed for inflation. In fact, the success of this system appears to have played a significant role in the continued expansion of the Colombian financial system (see the World Bank, 1987; and Barro, 1975).

Over the 1974 to 1984 period, for example, Colombia was one of the few Latin American countries that did not experience any significant reduction in broadly defined monetary assets as a share of GDP.[1] In contrast to most other Latin American countries, Colombian monetary balances continued to grow more rapidly than did the economy without any significant interruptions. It would be interesting to determine whether this more competitive and buoyant financial system reduced the costs of this factor of production by such an extent that it affected the level of economic growth.

Second, work on the sources of growth in Colombia, by Elias (1978) and Hanson *et al.* (1985), indicates that one of the larger 'unexplained' sources of growth in Colombia over the 1960–80 period occurred during the period when financial-sector policy innovations were introduced. Once again, it would be interesting to determine whether this higher level of technical change can be empirically related to the financial innovations.

Finally, the role that monetary balances may have played in economic growth in Colombia is of interest because indexed mortgages played a major role in this change in financial policy. Rather than deregulating the interest rate on deposits, and thereby simply permitting a more competitive market for broadly defined monetary balances, Colombia induced more competition. It did this by introducing indexed mortgages which provided higher yields on deposits than those available at commercial banks. In a sense, these indexed mortgages were similar to introducing a competitive Trojan Horse into the Colombian financial system. Other depository institutions had to compete with indexed mortgage lenders for deposits. The central way that they could do this was through paying more competitive interest rates on financial instruments. Over the 1972–84 period, for example, commercial bank certificates of deposit had an *ex post* average real return of 2.5 percent, after having yielded an average negative 6.5 percent real return for the previous 14 years.[2]

This kind of increased competition for funds may have a number of desirable allocative effects. However, it could also cause mortgage borrowers to 'crowd out' other investments, as suggested by Carrizosa *et al.* (1982). In many developing countries financial regulators proscribe the supplying of mortgages by the formal financial system because of this latter concern. In this respect, the study is one of the first attempts to analyze empirically the possible macroeconomic effects of providing households access to mortgage credit at competitive interest rates.

Keeping within the preliminary nature of the research, the econometric specification of the study is similar to the original Sinai and Stokes (1972) approach. Indeed, the approach taken is very much in the spirit of the original Solow (1957) article on aggregate production functions and the sources of growth. That is, we hope that we are not pushing the data beyond what can reasonably be inferred from such aggregate measures. Nevertheless, despite the more heuristic, rather than strictly quantitative nature of the analysis, we think that the results provide robust, if imprecise, evidence that a more competitive deposit and credit market played an important role in Colombia's economic growth.

The plan of the chapter is as follows. Section 7.2 reviews the effect that inflation can have on the cost of monetary balances and the way that indexation affects these costs. There then follows a description of the Colombian experience with regard to inflation, indexation, and increased financial competition. The effects of inflation on monetary aggregates and what we term 'equivalent units' of this factor of production are examined and compared to the levels that would have been obtained in the absence of indexation. In Section 7.3 the data and empirical results are presented and discussed. Section 7.4 reviews previous analyses of Colombian economic growth in light of the findings, and discusses the policy implications of our findings. Finally, section 7.5 summarizes.

7.2 INDEXED MONETARY BALANCES IN COLOMBIA

The Caha Ahorro Vivienda (CAVs), savings for housing institutions, were created in 1972 by a series of decrees by the Pastrana government. The government relied upon constitutional authority relating to the disposition of personal savings and their development played a major role in the government's development strategy.[3] Their design and implementation were placed under the direction of Lauchlin Currie.[4] These institutions were introduced into a financial system which had allocated a contracting share of national resources to the formal financial sector, and which operated parallel to a thriving and growing informal sector. For example, over the 1965–9 period credit outstanding as a share of GDP averaged 15 percent, whereas it averaged 19 percent in the preceding five-year period. In contrast, by the 1980–4 period, the net credit outstanding as a share of GDP averaged 36 percent, and there is indirect evidence that the level of economic activity in the informal sector had secularly contracted.[5]

As financial intermediaries, the CAVs represented both a liberalization and a further specialization of an already highly segmented and controlled financial system. They were a liberalization because they financed mortgages at positive *ex ante* real interest rates that were initially fully indexed for inflation, and they paid their depositors a similarly indexed real return. However, because they were the only intermediaries allowed to index both their credit and their liabilities to a unit of constant purchasing power, called UPACs, they were also a further specialization of the financial system. This specialization increased over time through a series of regulations that governed the share of the CAV portfolio. The regulations dictated the share of the portfolio that had to be lent for certain loan sizes, the interest rate that could be charged, and the permissible loan-to-value ratio of the various loan amounts. These directives were designed to insure that CAV lending was targeted towards lower- and moderate-income borrowers.

The return on CAV deposits was originally based on a three-month moving average, for the months immediately preceding the calculation, of the combined consumer price indices of blue- and white-collar workers. In 1987 the index was still changed daily with the quotations for the next month announced in advance. This method of indexation of the return on deposits means of course, that the index is based on the past rate of inflation, rather than a measure of inflation during the holding period for the deposit. It implies that an individual who deposits funds in a CAV knows with certainly the *nominal* rate of return, but not the *real* rate of return. Consequently, the central feature of indexation is not that the financial contract has immunized real returns from the effects of inflation. Rather, the chief features have been to create a system of deposits on which the interest rates gradually adjust to changes in the rate of inflation and provide a competitive real return to savers.

Such a system is hardly the idealized method of indexation that is recommended by economists (see Fischer, 1975). Nevertheless, these financial instrument have provided a means of avoiding most of the inflation tax on short-term financial assets and transaction balances, and as Barro (1975, p. 5) says they 'have induced some increases in the nominal interest rates paid on other financial assets. . . .' They have, in other words, lowered the costs of relying on the formal financial sector to provide a service that a formal sector institution should have a comparative advantage in providing.

An approximation of how Colombian policy reduced the effects of inflation on the costs of holding monetary balances can be made by computing a measure of the aggregate tax rate on monetary balances. Prior to the introduction of indexation, this tax applied to all monetary balances, because nominal interest rates on time deposits[6] were lower than the inflation rate and largely invariant to changes in it.[7] As a consequence, increases in the inflation rate affected the cost of $M1$, currency and demand deposits, as well as $M2$, which also includes time deposits. The tax on $M1$ is straightforward and in steady state is equal to $e(1+e)$, where e is the inflation rate.

For time deposits prior to the introduction of CAVs, the tax is more complicated. Because longer-term deposits yielded a negative real rate of return, the income to these assets was taxed at a 100 percent rate. But in addition, because the nominal return on these deposits, Rn, was always less than the inflation rate, these assets also lost value over time. Bringing all these effects together, the tax rate on what might be termed equivalent units of monetary balances can be described by:

$$T1 = \frac{\Theta}{(1 + \Theta)} \times \frac{M1}{Y} + \frac{(\Theta - Rn)}{(1 + (\Theta - Rn))} \times \frac{(M2 - M1)}{Y}$$
$$+ Rr \frac{(M2 - M1)}{Y} \tag{7.1}$$

where Rr is the real return on time deposits, and Y is GNP. The first and second terms on the right-hand side express the tax on monetary balances as the share of income that would be needed to restore these balances to their prior level. In other words, they represent taxes on the stock of $M1$ and $(M2 - M1)$ balances, respectively. The tax on real return on the non-$M1$ portion of the monetary balances is represented by the third term on the right-hand side.

Now consider how the introduction of indexed time and savings deposits affects this tax.[8] If the return on time deposits competes with the return on CAV time deposits, and this *real* return becomes invariant with respect to changes in the inflation rate, inflation would apply only to $M1$, and not at all to $M2$ or $M3$, which includes $M2$

plus CAV deposits. In this case the tax rate on monetary balances like Bailey's (1956) stylized descriptions of the inflation tax is:

$$T2 = \frac{\Theta}{(1 + \Theta)} \times \frac{M1}{Y} \qquad (7.2)$$

This kind of regulatory change eliminates both the inflation tax and loss of real return on non-$M1$ monetary balances. It also results in the inflation tax being applied only to $M1$ balances. In principle this is equivalent to assuming that the cost of the indexed balances is unaffected by changes in the inflation rate.

However, besides making the *real*, rather than the nominal, return on time deposits less variable with respect to changes in the inflation rate, the introduction of the CAVs also blurred the distinctions between the types of monetary balances. For example, Montenegro and Garcia (1986) found that after the introduction of indexation, the velocity of currency secularly increased. The continual decline in the share of $M1$ held in currency (from 31 percent in 1960 to less than 24 percent in 1974) was reversed. By 1984 the share of $M1$ held in currency had once again reached the level of 1960. They also found that the holdings of currency plus CAV savings deposits was without trend. They suggest that this latter result implies that CAV saving deposits became close substitutes for currency. In effect, CAV deposits became another vehicle through which the inflation tax could be avoided, and the costs of holding monetary balances reduced.

The presence of this vehicle significantly reduced the inflation tax both absolutely and relative to the inflation rate. The tax rate *per* percent of inflation is 0.166 percent in the former period and 0.116 percent in the latter period.[9] Some of the effects this reduction in the inflation tax rate and increase in the inflation rate had on the holdings of monetary balances is presented in Table 7.1.

In the pre-indexation period broadly-defined monetary balances, M, was a relatively constant share of GDP. In addition, the $M1$ share of total monetary balances showed an increasing trend. In the latter period, behavior was very different: $M1$ declined in importance (as a share of both GDP and M), as firms and households avoided the tax of the latter period's higher inflation rate. At the same time, broadly-defined monetary balances increased, as the re-

Table 7.1 Behavior of monetary aggregates and inflation over the
1958–84 period

Money aggregates	1958–72	1973–84
$\dot{M}1$/GDP	>0	<0
$\dot{M}$/GDP	0	>0
$M1/M$	.85	.57
$\dot{M}1/M$	>0	<0
θ	.110	.235

Note: The . indicates a derivative with respect to time. In the latter period, the coefficients were of an opposite sign from the former period and the standard errors were greatly reduced.

turns on these balances were better insulated from changes in the inflation rate.

To summarize, with the introduction of indexation, the Colombian financial system became competitive on the resource mobilization side. This competition for funds provided a way for households and firms to avoid much of the increase in the inflation tax on transaction balances. On the other hand, this system can hardly be described as a liberalized system that competitively allocates resources. As Correa (1986) documents, the assets of the system are still targeted to a wide range of below-market interest-rate loans in agriculture, industry, and low-income housing.[10]

A financial system that encourages more competition for deposits, and simultaneously requires lenders to make below market-rate loans, ultimately imposes the costs of the loans on the institutions rather than the depositors. Hence the financial crisis that began to affect the commercial banking system in 1982 is not surprising.[11] But this crisis was not the result of the increased competitiveness of the financial system. Rather, it is the incompleteness of the deregulation – particularly the restriction on lenders' asset powers – that created the problems.

7.3 THE MODEL AND THE DATA

A simple Cobb–Douglas production function with non-constant returns to scale is assumed and estimated in long-linear form. Like Sinai and Stokes (1972), we rely on single equation ordinary least squares estimation, corrected where necessary for autocorrelation. Our rationale for this single equation specification is twofold: first, the exploratory nature of our work; and second, the research subsequent to Sinai and Stokes' first article suggests that full information maximum likelihood, simultaneous equations, or two-stage least squares approaches do not result in significant changes in the estimated coefficients in any of the countries for which the functions have been estimated. See, for example, Sinai and Stokes (1977), and (1981), as well as Short (1979), and Khan and Ahmad (1985). Cumulatively, the work that has followed the original article suggests that OLS estimation is a reasonable approach. While we acknowledge the potentially substantial problems that could arise from simultaneity concerns, they are not dealt with here.[12]

The following equation was estimated with annual data over the 1958–84 period.

$$\ln GDP = \ln A + \alpha \ln K + \beta \ln L + \pi \ln M + u \qquad (7.3)$$

where:

GDP	=	total output
A	=	an efficiency parameter, the Greek letters are estimated parameters, and u is a disturbance term
K	=	capital
L	=	labor
M	=	equivalent units of real money balances

Data for output, labor, and capital were taken from a number of recent World Bank studies of the Colombian economy. Data on real output and the real capital stock were obtained from an update of a Harberger (1969) study of the Colombian capital stock. Data on real monetary balances are from the Banco de la Republica as reported in various World Bank documents. Employment data are from a Presidential Employment Mission, as reported in World Bank (1987).

They measure the number of persons in the labor force. This measure is a poorer measure of actual labor input that in hours worked but, as Romer (1987) indicates, it is at least symmetric with the measure of capital input.[13]

Our measure of equivalent units of monetary balances modifies the Sinai and Stokes' approach to account for the effects described in equations (7.1) and (7.2). To adjust for the more competitive yields on post-indexation time deposits, we assume that prior to indexation all monetary balances were taxed at the inflation rate, which is measured by the GDP deflator, and that after indexation was introduced in 1972, this tax applied only to $M1$. That is, after indexation was introduced time deposits yielded the market rate of interest and hence did not bear any inflation tax; and prior to the introduction of indexation both the $M1$ and $(M2 - M1)$ components of monetary balances were subject to the inflation tax as described in equation (7.1).[14] See appendix in section 7.6 for a complete description of all the variables.

Table 7.2 presents the results of the estimated equations with and without monetary balances. Equation (7.4) indicates that a standard Cobb–Douglas production function without monetary balances describes the Colombian data fairly well. The returns to scale – 1.4 – and the output elasticities – labor 68 percent and capital 51 percent – are similar to the results of Khan and Ahmad (1985) for Pakistan. They found returns to scale of 1.33 without money balances and elasticities of 75 percent and 58 percent, respectively. Sinai and Stokes (1972) also reported increasing returns to scale for the US: 1.78. Although their output elasticities (1.36 and 0.43, respectively) were very different from ours, these kinds of differences between developed and developing countries – in particular a much higher relative elasticity for capital in developing economies – are consistent with Elias' (1978) findings for Latin America.

All but one of the coefficients in equations (7.4)–(7.7) in the table are significant at the 5 percent level (the labor coefficient in equation 5 is significant at the 10 percent level). The standard error of equation (7.4) without correction for auto-correlation, .047, is larger than the Sinai and Stokes (1972) estimate (.034) for a much longer period with superior input measures for the US. Equations (7.5)–(7.7) show that whether defined as $M1$, $M2$, or $M3$, real monetary balances are of substantial statistical importance. The standard error

Table 7.2 Estimates of the parameters of the Cobb–Douglas production
function, with and without real money balances, corrected for
autocorrelation, for the years 1958–84

LN GDP = LN A + Alpha* LN K + BETA* LN L + GAMMA* LN M + U				
Regression with:---	NO MONEY (7.4)	NEW1 (7.5)	NEW2 (7.6)	NEW3 (7.7)
LN A	−4.76	−1.78	−0.03	−0.78
	(.694)	(.613)	(1.189)	(1.543)
A	0.0086	0.1686	0.9704	0.4584
ALPHA	0.51	0.16	0.32	0.43
	(0.123)	(.101)	(.132)	(.136)
BETA	0.89	0.83	0.48	0.49
	(.182)	(.139)	(.215)	(.261)
GAMMA	-------	0.37	0.36	0.23
		(0.36)	(.065)	(.066)
SUMMATION	1.4	1.36	1.16	1.15
R-SQ (a)	0.9866	0.9975	0.9939	0.9914
SEE (b)	0.047	0.021	0.032	0.04
DW (c)	1.742	1.673	1.506	1.648

Note: Standard errors of regression coefficients are in parentheses.
(a): Adjusted R-square (R-SQ) for equation not corrected for autocorrelation.
(b): Standard error of estimation (SEE) for equation not corrected for autocorrelation.
(c): Durbin–Watson (DW) Statistic for equation corrected for autocorrelation.

of the equation uncorrected for auto-correlation is reduced in every
case: to .021 for the equation including $M1$, .032 for the equation
including $M2$ and .04 for the equation including $M3$. In addition,
estimates of equations that were not corrected for auto-correlation
indicate that there is much less of a problem in this respect in equations
(7.5)–(7.7), than there is in equation (7.4), as would be expected if
monetary balances were an omitted variable in equation 4.[15]

　　The coefficients on our measures of monetary balances ranged
from .23 to .37. These results are somewhat higher than those of
Sinai and Stokes' (.17 to .21), and somewhat lower than Khan and
Ahmad's for M1, .43. Adding $M1$ to the equation did not significantly affect the returns to scale, whereas adding $M2$ or $M3$ did.
The latter variables also reduced the contribution of labor by a much
greater amount, as is the case in previous research. Similarly, the
pattern of change in coefficients when monetary balances are added
to the estimated function is qualitatively similar to those of Sinai

Table 7.3   Estimates of the parameters of the Cobb–Douglas production
function, with real money balances (with and without adjustment for
indexation and inflation)
corrected for autocorrelation, for the years 1958–84

$LN\ GDP = LN\ A + ALPHA* LN\ K + BETA* LN\ L + GAMMA* LN\ M + u$		
	SOL2	NEW2
	(7.8)	(7.9)
LN A	−0.61	−0.03
	(1.506)	(1.189)
A	0.5434	0.9704
ALPHA	0.34	0.32
	(.161)	(.132)
BETA	0.54	0.48
	(.234)	(.215)
GAMMA	0.34	0.36
	(.107)	(.065)
SUMMATION	1.22	1.16
R-SQ (a)	0.9918	0.9939
SEE (b)	0.037	0.032
DW (c)	1.793	1.506

Note: Standard errors of regression coefficients are in parentheses.
(a): Adjusted R-square (R-SQ) for equation not corrected for autocorrelation.
(b): Standard error of estimation (see) for equation not corrected for autocorrelation.
(c): Durbin–Watson (DW) Statistic for equation corrected for autocorrelation.

and Stokes (see Table 7.3).

Table 7.3 compares estimates of equation (7.3) without adjustment of monetary balances (*M*2) for equivalent units such as those
of Sinai and Stokes with our adjusted measure of *M*2 from Table
7.2. A comparison of the results indicates that the adjustment to
account for the inflation taxes on monetary balances improves the
explanatory power of our estimation without having much effect on
the coefficients of labor or capital. The SEE (standard error of estimation) is lower in the equation where equivalent units of *M*2 are
used and the coefficients are better confirmed.

To summarize, like previous studies, our estimates suggest that
monetary balances have played an important role in Colombian economic growth and therefore should be included in analyses of the
sources of growth. We realize that our input data are clearly far
from perfect, and even our measure of the effect of the changes in

the tax structure in the measurement of monetary balances, will not achieve Jorgenson and Griliches' (1967) aspiration of eliminating the residual, through better measurement of the inputs. Nevertheless, the robustness of our estimates under various input definitions is at least suggestive that our findings are not adventitious. Solow's (1988) recent comment on this topic helps put our results in perspective:

> Thus technology remains the dominant engine of growth, with human capital second. One does not have to believe in the accuracy of these numbers; the message they transmit is pretty clear anyway. That is meant as a serious remark, every piece of empirical economics rests on a substructure of background assumptions that are probably not quite true. Under those circumstances, robustness should be the supreme economic virtue; . . . so I would be happy if you were to accept the results I have been quoting to point to a qualitative truth and perhaps give some guide to orders of magnitude. (Solow 1988, p. 314)

7.4   THE AUGMENTED PRODUCTION FUNCTION AND OTHER STUDIES OF COLOMBIAN ECONOMIC GROWTH

We focus on three of the many issues that have been raised in the extensive literature on Colombian growth: (1) Has the introduction of indexed mortgage instruments affected economic growth? (2) Can we draw any conclusions about the effect of financial policy on income distribution? and (3) Are there any additional potential 'source of growth' type problems that can be identified by the inclusion of monetary balances as a factor of production?

Indexation and Economic Growth

Carrizosa *et al.* (1982) have argued that the introduction of indexation had little effect on the level of economic growth. They suggest that because of credit fungibility, the central effect of increasing formal-sector mortgage financing was a substitution of financing from alternative sources of funds. This point of view has been contended by Currie and Rosas (1986) who argue that mortgage indexation played an important part in Colombia's economic growth by stimulating housing as a lead sector in the economy.

Whether mortgage indexation led to an increased growth rate, particularly in the manner described by Currie (1974), is perhaps an intractable econometric question. Although the lower average level of GDP invested in housing after the introduction of indexation does provide some support to the credit fungibility argument raised by Carrizosa *et al.* (1982). Our analysis suggests a different channel through which the introduction of mortgage indexation might have indirectly affected growth: by stimulating the competition for financial resources, they helped reduce the burden of inflationary taxes on monetary balances. This effect, in turn, led to a reduction in the costs of an important factor of production. According to this perspective, this cost reduction facilitated investment rather than affected its composition, and thereby affected growth.

To get an approximation of the effects of financial technology on overall growth, it is convenient to assume that the production function is linearly homogenous, and that the necessary conditions for producer equilibrium apply. With these assumptions output elasticities sum to one, and the effect of the estimated increasing returns to scale on total factor productivity is eliminated. Comparing the adjusted coefficients from linearized versions of equations (7.4) and (7.6), that is, production functions with and without monetary balances, we find that in equation (7.4) technical change, or in Abramovitz's terms, the measure of our ignorance, accounts for 72 percent of growth in total factor productivity. In equation (7.6), in contrast, technical change accounts for only 35 percent of the growth in total factor productivity.[16] The inclusion of monetary balances has cut the unexplained residual in half. Hence, even if our coefficients are off by a factor of two, it appears inescapable that the change in the structure of financial technology has made a very substantial contribution to economic growth in Colombia.

Income Distribution Issues

Measuring the incidence of lower inflationary taxes on a more competitive financial system is, as Urrutia (1985) shows, a very difficult task, and our aggregate results shed little direct light on this important issue. Rather than trying to tease out the possible effects that financial policy may have had on income or wealth distribution, as Berry and Soligo (1980) have creatively done, it is perhaps of more interest to consider briefly, in the words of Sherlock Holmes, 'a dog that did not bark'. The dog in this case is the observation that the share of income of the lowest-income group did not deteriorate over the 1958–84 period. In fact, it improved.[17] The improvement is surprising because the traditional view of the development process is that during development there is generally an initial deterioration in the earnings of lower-income groups. Chenery and Syrquin's (1975) model allows for a rough quantification of how income level shares might be expected to behave.[18] It indicates that, based on Colombia's income level and population growth over this period, a slight deterioration in the share of income in the lowest two quintals was to be expected.[19]

The interesting aspect of the somewhat surprising improvement in the relative position of the poor, is that one of the chief reasons for proscribing market-rate housing finance systems in developing countries is the concern that these systems will not serve the poor. Rather, it is argued, they will lead to a deterioration in the position of the poor. See, for example, World Bank (1980). Indeed, in many countries the reliance on the housing finance system to provide 'affordable', that is, very low nominal interest rates, is a direct result of distributional considerations prompted by concerns about the presumed unaffordability of market-rate mortgage credit.

We are not suggesting that mortgage indexation was a cause of observed distributional results. Factors other than housing finance policy or financial policy clearly have more to do with the observed trends in income distribution. Nevertheless, the Colombian case is interesting in that it suggests that the development of market-oriented housing finance systems can make a significant contribution to economic growth contemporaneously with an improvement in the position of the lowest-income groups. Hence, it does not appear that greater access to mortgage credit by moderate and upper-income households is antithetical to the interests of the poor.

Financial Policy and the Sources of Growth

Perhaps the most appropriate standard against which to evaluate the usefulness of including monetary balances in the production function, is whether it yields any insights about the sources of growth not suggested by the traditional growth-accounting perspective. The augmented production function performs well on this score. The inclusion of monetary balances suggests an important channel through which macroeconomic financial policy can affect growth: the channel is the effect of the level of inflation on the competitiveness of the resource mobilization process.

Since 1984, the last year of our estimation period, an interest-rate cap has been placed on mortgage indexation so that the adjustment has been below the rate of inflation. As a result, since that time the mortgages supplied – which now account for 25 percent of financial assets – provide lenders less protection against increases in the inflation rate. If inflation increases, lenders will be unable to increase borrowers' repayment by as much. Hence, these instruments will not provide the CAVs a means of competing for deposits. As a result, the CAVs will either (1) be unable to compete for funds with commercial banks and suffer disintermediation; or (2) if the banks do not compete for funds with the CAVs, the overall competitiveness of the deposit system will be greatly reduced. In either case the cost of this factor of production will increase substantially.

For example, because of the ceiling on indexation an increase in inflation would act like a tax on *all* monetary balances, not just $M1$. As a consequence, a 10 percent increase in the rate of inflation (from 25 percent to about 35 percent) would result in pushing up the cost of $M1$. But, in addition, the tax would apply to all monetary balances. The tax base would more than double. Hence, the augmented production-function permits the effects of increase in the inflation rate to be traced through to its effect on growth. Again, while this kind of quantification of the effects is stylized, it nevertheless is a clear channel through which the inflation and the current financial regulatory environment can very significantly affect growth. Moreover, it is a channel ignored by standard sources of growth analyses.

7.5   CONCLUSION

The role of financial policy in economic growth is always a difficult one to quantify. For an economy, such as Colombia, in which
trade policy changes and illegal exports have played important roles,
this comment carries even more weight. Nevertheless, the empirical
approach developed by Sinai and Stokes (1977) is a helpful framework within which some of the more important financial development policy issues can be considered and broadly quantified. While
caution should clearly be applied to interpretations of the coefficients, the results strongly suggest that financial policy has played
an important role in Colombia's record of sustained growth.

A central component of this policy has been the ability to finance
investments in the 'unproductive' and socially meretricious portion
of the housing stock, that is, the portion of housing production not
allocated to the poor. However, importantly, our results indicate that
it was not the effects of finance on the composition of investment
patterns that mattered. Rather, growth was stimulated by not only
permitting, but inducing, the financial system to be able to minimize the effects of high and variable inflation rates on the cost of
monetary balances. Household access to credit for 'low priority'
investments played an important part in the process of including a
cost-reducing, more competitive financial technology. While it does
not appear that the forced investment schemes that still litter the
financial system have made the best use of the resources mobilized
by the more competitive deposit system, one can only speculate
about what would have occurred if the resources were not in the
financial system at all.

7.6   APPENDIX

Explanation of Variables

GDP: Gross Domestic Product in 1980 Colombian billion pesos.
K: The capital series is from Harberger and is in 1980 Colombian
           billion pesos.
L: The number of persons in the labor force and is in 1000s.
*NEW*1:   Equivalent units of monetary balances are defined as $M1$ in bil-
           lions ($M1$) of 1980 pesos, adjusted for inflation and indexation as
           follows:

$NEW1 = m1 \dfrac{*\ 1}{(1-\Theta)}$, where $m1$ is the real monetary balance, and Θ is the inflation rate. Hence, $(1/1-\Theta)$ acts as a measure of the change in the number of equivalent units of monetary balances due to a change in the inflation rate.

$NEW2$: Equivalent units of monetary balances defined as $M2$
$(M2)$ with the same $(M2)$ adjustments made as $M1$ prior to 1973. From 1973 onwards, no adjustment is made for inflation and indexation, that is, pre-1973, $NEW2 = I/(1-\Theta)^* \ m2$, where $m2$ is real monetary balances; 1973 and after: $NEW2 = I/(1-\Theta)^* \ m1 + (m2 - m1)$. This means that the equivalent units of the non-M1 portion of monetary balances are unaffected by changes in the inflation rate. Indexation was introduced in the fourth quarter of 1972.

$NEW3$: Equivalent units of monetary balances defined as $M2$ and $M3$.
$(M3)$ *CAV* deposits $(M3)$ starting from 1973. The change in equivalent units of $(M3-M2)$ is the same as that of $(M2-M1)$.

$SOL1$: $M1$ in real terms.
$SOL2$: $M2$ in real terms.
$SOL3$: $M2 + CAV$ in real terms.
Note: The inflation rate was derived from the GNP deflator.

8 The Fiscal Policy Dimension: Implicit Subsidies

8.1 INTRODUCTION

This chapter examines the kinds of housing subsidies that are often channeled through housing finance systems in economies experiencing high inflation and financial stress. Argentina in the late 1980s is used as a case study. However, the kinds of programs analyzed appear to be very similar to the programs in operation in a number of other economies.[1] The purpose of the chapter is twofold.

First, it presents simple measures of both the subsidy level and welfare costs of housing policy. A user cost-of-capital approach is used to measure the subsidy level. The main advantages of this approach are that it shows first, how sensitive the subsidy level can be to general housing market conditions, and second, how such conditions can cause the size and efficiency of the subsidy to be very different from those suggested by traditional budgetary measures. These implicit credit subsidies have not been measured by traditional fiscal accounting measures. The unmeasured subsidies are very large and the present value of welfare losses is ever larger; the latter may be as high as 6 percent of GDP.

Second, the chapter provides a preliminary and seemingly paradoxical answer to the question: 'Who should be first in the housing subsidy queue?' In an economy as disrupted as Argentina's, the answer is not the obvious one: that is should be those who have the most housing need, however that is defined. In this economy many high-return housing investments are foregone because of policies that impede formal financial intermediation, increasing its costs and reducing its availability. Corresponding to this contraction in the availability of credit has been a similar contraction in both the stock and production of housing. At the same time that the total supply of housing has been contracting, real rents, like real borrowing costs, have increased sharply. In many respects, Argentina's housing market appears to be functioning much like its financial system. However, unlike the effects of a shrinking formal financial system – that is, increased consumption or capital flight – a contracting housing market can impose high costs on most lower-income families.

One way of reducing these costs is to target much smaller subsidies on those willing to mobilize their own resources. Such a subsidy distribution takes into account the value of the subsidy to the beneficiary rather than just the cost to the government. It can be expected to have a much larger effect on net housing investment than does the current method of targeting very large subsidies on those least able to afford housing.

The current subsidy approach redistributes wealth but has little effect on output. Providing subsidies to those lower-income households willing and able to mobilize some resources could significantly increase the housing production induced by the subsidy. A large increase in production could lower rents for all renters, rather than lower the cost of housing for the small portion of eligible families that the program can reach directly. Hence, it appears that the best way to provide the most housing assistance to the poor is not to target the subsidies exclusively on those who are the poorest.

Ultimately, questions such as: how many new housing units can be induced by a given government expenditure? and, what is the effect of housing production on rent levels? are difficult empirical matters that are not answered in this chapter. The aims here are more modest. They are: (1) showing that it is important to consider, if not measure, the indirect effects that housing subsidies can have; and (2) demonstrating that subsidy allocation schemes that consider only the cost and not the value of the subsidy are likely to be inefficient.

The plan of the chapter is as follows. In Section 8.2 the Argentine economic crisis, the major housing-finance institutions, and housing-market conditions are briefly described. Then, in Sections 8.3 and 8.4 user-cost estimates of the effects of various housing and financial policies are presented. Section 8.5 provides a measure of the resource costs to the economy of these policies and a measure of the scale of the implicit taxes that have financed the transfers. A final section summarizes.

8.2   RECENT ECONOMIC AND HOUSING-MARKET TRENDS IN ARGENTINA

The Economy

Argentina is a highly urbanized country with one of the most uniform distributions of income in Latin America. In 1980, 83 percent of the population was living in urban areas. Over the preceding 20 years approximately 11 percent of the population had moved from a rural to urban location. Its housing market is predominately owner-occupied (62 percent), and one that in 1976 had just emerged from 40 years of binding rent control. The late 1970s also saw the emergence of indexed mortgage loans. Prior to this time mortgage credit was provided at low fixed rates, despite inflation rates of 20 to 30 percent per year.[2]

Argentina has also experienced a deep and sustained reduction in real income, very high real borrowing rates, the highest average inflation rate in the world for the 1975–85 period, and capital flight of significant scale.[3] Over the 1975–84 period, real *per capita* income fell by more than 20 percent to approximately $2 100 *per capita*. The size of the formal financial system contracted sharply with the extension of regulated interest-rate ceiling on deposits. Despite such interest-rate ceilings, real borrowing costs have been higher than 30 percent per year, even though deposit rates were deeply negative over much of this period. Net investment (and particularly housing investment) has also been very low.[4]

The Housing Sector

Against such a background it is not surprising that the public-sector share of housing units produced almost doubled (going from 28 percent in 1979 to about 50 percent in 1985), as the unsubsidized demand for housing should certainly fall in such an environment. Nor is it surprising that long-term credit should contract, and long-lived investments such as housing should be deferred. What is surprising is the level of disruption in the housing market. For the 1982–5 period, housing production was significantly below the rate of household formation expected by the growth of population and was almost certainly negative on a net of depreciation basis.[5]

In addition to a limited flow of new production, the services provided by the stock of existing housing also contracted. For example, in 1985 the supply of housing units for rent in Greater Buenos Aires, a market that accounts for over 40 percent of the national rental market, was 25 percent less than the 1980 figure. Owners of housing units that could have been offered for rent, apparently felt that unoccupied units were preferable. Even though real rent and real rent-to-house value ratios in Greater Buenos Aires and other cities increased significantly, the supply of units for rent contracted.[6] Hence, from an aggregate perspective, the flow of new housing units was insufficient to satisfy the flow of net new households, and the stock of existing units also contracted, as units were taken off the market.

The House Subsidy System

Almost all housing finance in Argentina is provided through two instruments: an earmarked wage tax fund (the National Housing Fund, FONAVI), and a National Mortgage Bank (BHN). Since the late 1970s public housing has been funded mainly by FONAVI. In 1986, the tax was estimated to yield the equivalent of about 1.4 percent of GDP. The tax has provided funding for over 70 percent of subsidized housing produced over the 1980–5 period. FONAVI beneficiaries had an average *per capita* income of about US$750, significantly below the *per capita* income level of US$2 100, and the housing units produced cost 18 300 australs, or almost US$17 000.[7]

FONAVI's ability to recover resources is hampered by poor recovery of the real value of the money it lends. Even though households tend to make repayments, because of the lending terms and the high rate of inflation only a small fraction of the real value of FONAVI expenditures, on the order of 2 to 5 percent, is ever re covered by FONAVI.[8]

The National Mortgage Bank (BHN) is the chief alternative source of funds. It also provides credit subsidies. At the beginning of 1987, it was the third large financial intermediary in the country with a US$1.8 billion portfolio, comprised almost completely of indexed mortgage loans. BHN has evolved from being a bank that had generated about half of its funds from internal sources to one that had a negative cash-flow. It was maintained by US$1 billion in loans from the Central Bank of Argentina and the deposits of public agencies that yielded deeply negative interest rates.[9] There is almost no other credit available for house purchase and there are no other subsidies. Throughout the 1980s almost all other housing sales in Buenos Aires were made with cash in US dollars, and the price of housing oscillated mildly around a rising trend that was far less volatile than the behavior of Argentine stock market indices.[10]

To summarize, housing market data suggest a contracting market. Sustained increases in rent-to-house value ratios do not elicit either net new production, or expansion of the supply of existing rental housing. Significant resource transfers to the sector through FONAVI and BHN (1.5 to 2 percent of GDP) appear to induce little incremental private expenditures on housing. Perhaps most importantly, as is explained in the next section, the expected present value of the flow of housing services exceeds the cost of production by a significant amount, suggesting a market in disequilibrium. The next section discusses how housing and financial policies intersect to create and sustain this disequilibrium, and how its sustainment effects the efficiency of the resources transferred to the sector.

8.3 A USER-COST OF CAPITAL APPROACH TO THE HOUSING MARKET

To measure the scale of the transfers and the costs of a possible disequilibrium of the housing market, disequilibrium must first be defined. Suppose initially that there are low costs of shifting between supplying housing services to oneself, or to another consumer. In this case the value of a house, Pk, is the same whether it is owned or rented, and its value is equal to both the expected flow of services yielded by the asset – that is, the house, and the cost of supplying the asset, Pc. Discrepancies between Pk and Pc induce investment of disinvestment. Disequilibrium occurs if Pk remains above Pc for an extended period of time without inducing more investment in housing, as has occurred in Argentina.

One straightforward explanation for the disequilibrium is: there is no forward market in rental housing but there is one in owner-occupied housing. If landlords are at all uncertain about their ability to collect rents because of fear, among other things, of the re-imposition of rent control, they will demand a premium for bearing this risk. Consequently, the supply of rental housing services shifts to the left by more than the shift in the supply of owner-occupied housing services. This premium causes rent-to-house value ratios to rise, increasing the cost of renting relative to owning a house. These higher rents can be avoided only by becoming a home-owner. However, because new construction levels are at such low levels, this demand for home-ownership must be met from the existing stock; for example, converting rental units. Consequently, the supply of rental housing decreases as landlords keep their units vacant to be able to sell to those who can afford to buy rather than rent. The result is yet an additional increase in rent-to-house value ratios, as the supply of rental housing supply curve shifts further to the left.

The presence of a forward market in only the owner-occupied part of the housing market, together with severe constraints on new housing investment, is one way that a disequilibrium could occur in the Argentine housing market. It is, of course, not the only way. For example, virtually all econometric models of the far less fragmented US and UK housing markets rely on the disequilibrium specifications.[11] Hence, the argument is not so much that the specific nature of the disequilibrium is clear, but rather that there is evidence that the Argentine housing market can be characterized as having been in disequilibrium for an extended period of time.

In order to measure how much Pk had diverged from Pc, I analyze the determinants of Pk and consider how they have changed over time. For example, if Pk were determined solely by taking the present value of expected rents, then assumptions about the expected real rents and the equally unobservable real discount rate would yield a measure of Pk. Because the real interest rate is not observable, this kind of computation becomes complicated. An even more important computational problem arises because housing provides more than just shelter services. Like other forms of capital, it also provides a store of value for savings, a service that can play an increasingly important role in evaluating the behavior of housing investment under inflationary conditions. This type of return depends upon the returns to the alternative savings instruments available.

Because of the unobservable discount rates and returns, we are left with a computation for the present value of user-cost of FONAVI housing units that is a stylized figure. Nevertheless, such stylized measures have a number of significant advantages. First, such synthetic measures underlie almost all empirical studies of investment behavior. Consequently, the construction of such stylized figures is simply an extension of empirical investment analysis to housing investments. Indeed, almost all recent empirical analyses of housing investment use such an approach.

Second, the user-cost approach provides a simple and manageable measure of the form and level of government intrusion into the credit markets that is implied by a particular financial process. It provides a measure of the *ex ante* subsidy and/or contingent liability implied by a particular policy. In an economy in which a large share of government resources is channeled through the financial system, the development of such measures are prerequisite to the control of government's command over resources and risk exposure. In this respect, the approach is very similar to the new budgetary measures applied to the US credit budget, and the demonstration of the applicability of the technique is more important than the particular estimates made.[12] Moreover, as is shown below, the subsidy level implied by the user-cost approach is very different from that of traditional budgetary measures.

Third, empirical studies of Argentina by Diaz-Alejandro (1970) and Mallon and Sourrouville (1975) both argue that one of the most serious failings of government policy in Argentina has been the way that various policies have increased the relative price of the existing capital stock. They estimate that if capital formation figures through the 1960s were adjusted to reflect the relative prices of capital goods, these figures would be reduced by as much as 30 percent. Applying a user cost-of-capital perspective to the housing sector is very much in the spirit of these analyses. Indeed, its application is the kind of extension of this earlier work that is necessary to give their empirical conjectures analytic and policy content.

To sum up, user-cost measures of transfers are likely to be more accurate than are cost-of-production measures whenever the relevant markets are characterized by disequilibrium. They are also likely to be helpful in understanding the scale of transfers whenever the transfer is provided through a segmented financial system in which prices do not clear markets. Finally, as is shown in the next section, these measures can also be very helpful in targeting subsidies to improve their efficiency.

8.4   APPLYING THE USER-COST APPROACH TO THE ARGENTINE HOUSING MARKET

Laidler's (1969) approach is used to decompose the effect of various policies on housing's asset price. It is easiest to begin from the case of equilibrium and then proceed to introduce the effects of various policies which affect the relationship between the cost and value of a housing unit.

The Equilibrium Case

For a house costing 18 000 australs to produce, and situated on land worth approximately 6 000 australs (as was the case for FONAVI units), assume that the mortgage payments of beneficiaries are equal to 20 percent of household initial income of 4000 australs per year. Annual payments then are equal to 800 australs per year. Assume also that payments are maintained in real terms by loan indexation and paid in a timely fashion. In this case, the present value of the repayments equals 10 500 australs. The difference between the present value of the loan repayment and the value of the house is the amount of subsidy the household receives. It is equal to about 13 500 australs, or 56 percent of the value of the house. Because FONAVI pays for the structure, but not the land, which is contributed at zero cost, it gives a net subsidy equal to 42 percent (18 000 – 10 500) of its expenditures, and 56 percent (7 500/13 500) of the net transfer the household receives. These figures are shown in bar I of Figures 8.1A and 8.1B (the numbers are rounded off).

These levels of subsidy would apply if Pk equals Pc.[13] These assumed equilibrium housing-market conditions obviously are very different from the Argentine housing-market conditions described earlier. Now consider how various aspects of Argentine housing- and financial-market conditions affect the scale of the disequilibrium, and hence the difference between the size of the transfer and the cost of the subsidy.

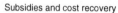

(a) PV of FONAVI house & mortgage payment
(Figures in Thousand Australs)

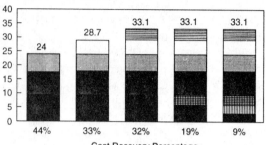

(b) FONAVI subsidy as a share of total resource transfer
(Figures in Thousand Australs)

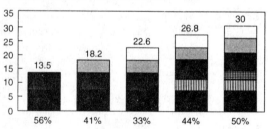

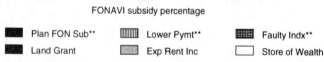

** indicates FONAVI subsidy.

Figure 8.1a

Cost Rec:	Cost recovery from the borrowers.
Faulty Indx:	Faulty indexation which distorts the interest rate charged.
Lower Pymt:	Lower payments by borrowers.
Plan FONAVI Sub:	Planned FONAVI subsidy, that is, original level of subsidy planned by FONAVI.
Land Don:	Land Donation.
Ex Rent Inc:	Expected rent increases in the future years.
Store of Wealth:	Store of wealth for the borrowers.

Figure 8.1b

Plan FON Sub**:	Planned FONAVI subsidy.
Lower Pymt**:	Lower payments – FONAVI subsidy.
Faulty Indx**:	Faulty indexation – FONAVI Subsidy.
Land Grant:	Land grant – FONAVI subsidy.
Exp Rent Inc:	Expected rent increases – not a FONAVI subsidy.
Store of Wealth:	Store of wealth – not a FONAVI subsidy.

Figure 8.1   Housing-finance subsidies in Argentina

The Effects of High Real Interest Rates, and Increasing Real Rents on Housing Valuation

A number of studies have reported that real borrowing costs in the Argentine financial system exceeded 30 percent during the 1980s. If a 30 percent discount rate were used to evaluate housing investment decisions, even a 20 percent *per annum* increase in real rents would result in disinvestment in housing. However, as documented by Khan and Ul Hague (1987), significant amounts of Argentine capital have fled the country to invest at real international interest rates that, according to Hendershott (1984), ranged from 2 to 5.5 percent during this period. Beside making investments abroad, Argentines also made dollar-denominated investments in non-subsidized housing within Argentina. The opportunity-cost of these investments is the real international interest rate, less transaction costs. As a result, if there were credible formal financial intermediaries in Argentina, funds could be borrowed at the same real interest rate at which Argentines are investing them abroad.

In this perspective the higher costs are, in effect, selective credit policies that drive tax-like wedges into the evaluation of the value of investments in different sectors of the economy. The size of these wedges is in direct proportion to sector's reliance on the financial system. To quantify these effects, housing returns were discounted at an interest rate that reflected the real international cost of funds and the 'technological' costs of the kind of intermediation performed (that is, the underwriting and administration). I assume that this discount rate is equal to 6.5 percent, inclusive of a 2.5 percent transaction cost of intermediating. Then the pre-tax value of housing is compared with the observed cost of producing such an investment, that is, the FONAVI per-unit cost. The difference between these figures, that is $Pk - Pc$, provides a measures of the profitability of housing investment foregone, due to policies which obstruct savings from moving to high-return investments.

The first step in determining Pk is to generate a measure of expected rents. I assume that the expected returns to housing are determined by a distributed lag process that takes into account past increases in rents and real interest rates. I also assume that the Argentine experience causes households to expect to have an annual rent increase of from 8 to 10 percent of house price.[14] The second step is to assume an economic depreciation rate for the house. Like the equilibrium case and the Argentine trends, I assume constant real house value. With these assumptions, households who gain access to a FONAVI house receive housing services, a wealth transfer, and a forward financial transaction. The last occurs because households expect that the increase in rent-to-value ratios will not induce an increase of sufficient scale in the housing supply to reduce this ratio to its former level. Access to ownership affords households a way to avoid expected future real rent increases. Under the assumption of an increase in the rent-to-house value ratio of from 8 to 10 percent of house value, the present value increases by 4 700 australs. This figure is in addition to the 18 800 australs of rental services flowing from an 8 percent annual net rental value. In other words, the value of avoiding the expected rent increases, that is, the value of the forward transaction, equals 19 percent of the housing unit's value.

The estimated total resource transfer in this case is 28 700 australs. Under these circumstances, subtracting the present value of the mortgage repayments yields a net resource transfer equal to approximately 18 200 australs. This amount is more than 100 percent of the assumed FONAVI expenditures, even though by fiscal accounting measures FONAVI provides a subsidy that is equal to only 42 percent of its expenditures. These effects are shown in bar II in Figures 8.1A and 8.1B.

It is likely that the extremely high, real borrowing-costs are a major contributing factor to housing production's failure to respond to the increasing real rents. However, these higher real borrowing-costs are not the only implicit tax imposed on households. Besides having to pay more to borrow and rent, these households also receive negative returns on their savings as long as the savings are held in regulated financial assets. This kind of regulatory tax also effects the value placed on housing as a store of wealth.

The Effects of a Repressed Financial System on Housing Valuation

Apart from housing, few other forms of domestic savings maintained their real value during the 1978–85 period. Hence, *ex post* housing was a relatively attractive form of domestic savings. If interest-rate ceilings on deposits interacted with inflation to reduce households' discount rate in such a way that the *ex ante* real opportunity cost of funds was 2 percent rather than 4 percent, as was assumed earlier,[15] then the present value of the house increases from 28 700 to 31 100 australs. This is shown in bar III of Figures 8.1A and 8.1B. The net resource transfer of the FONAVI subsidy (18 000–10 500) measures about one-third of the subsidy the household receives (31 100–10 500). The per-unit subsidy increases by almost 9 000 australs relative to what it would have been in housing and credit markets that were not in disequilibrium, that is, the equilibrium case. In effect, the interaction of inflation and interest-rate ceilings increased the steady-state demand for housing as an asset of refuge. Simultaneously, through increasing real borrowing-cost to extraordinary levels, credit policy reduced the ability of the economy to fulfill this demand.

The Effects of the Subsidy Program Structure

Ex ante subsidy problems

To this point it has been assumed that FONAVI loan repayments are indexed for inflation and are equal to 20 percent of initial household income. In fact, initial payments have averaged only about 12 percent of income. As a result, the *ex ante* per-unit subsidy is larger. Due to this change, the present value of mortgage repayments to FONAVI falls from 10 500 australs to 6 300 australs, and the FONAVI subsidy rate goes from about 40 percent of its expenditures to more than 65 percent. This is shown in bars IV in Figures 8.1A and 8.1B. This larger per-unit subsidy allows lower-income households to afford payments. In principle, at least, it enables the subsidy to be targeted towards those with the most housing need. As a result, of course, fewer of the many eligible households can be helped. But before addressing this important targeting problem, another subsidy must first be identified.

Ex post subsidy problems

Although not emphasized in Figure 8.1, one of the most important subsidies is given through the repayment index scheme. FONAVI mortgage payments are indexed to wages and not inflation. As a result, the lender, FONAVI, bears real-income risk. If real income falls, mortgage payments do not increase as rapidly as does inflation. In many cases, payments even a few years after loan origination represent only a tiny share of income. For example, the average loan repayment received by FONAVI in 1985 was equal to one fifth of 1 percent of house value, or 36 australs per year. In effect, the repayment indexes 'over-protect' already heavily subsidized households from the real-income shocks of the macroeconomic environment.

Providing some form of insurance or protection for borrowers may be a reasonable strategy in an economy where real-income growth is uncertain, and interest rates have reached such high and volatile levels. However, the Argentine approach is very expensive. The indices and repayment terms used by FONAVI provide more than complete insulation from interest-rate or real-income risks. Under its scheme the small number of households who are lucky enough to gain access to housing assistance are insulated from economic shocks. Indeed, their position has improved substantially when economic growth falters, or inflation increases.

The repayment scheme effectively provides real-wage insurance for wage reductions that may affect the more than 200 000 families with outstanding loans.[16] Unfortunately, the benefits of this insurance become operative regardless of the behavior of household income. If, for instance, a FONAVI beneficiary experienced an increase in real income at the same time that there was a reduction in the aggregate minimum-wage index, his real payments would still be reduced because of the index used. This indirect form of insurance against reductions in real wages is not targeted on those who need it.

To approximate the effects of partial indexation for inflation on the size of the per-unit subsidy, assume that throughout the life of the loan, real payments are expected to decline in such a way that the average payment is half of what it would have been if indexation adjusted for changes in the inflation rate. As a consequence, expected annual payments are equal to 6 percent of initial income rate than the initial 12 percent, or 240/18 000 = .013 of house price per year. This figure, 1.3 percent of house price, is 1.2 percent lower than the 2.5 percent year administrative costs of operating the program.

In this case, the subsidy is equal to: (1) the entire imputed rental value of the housing units, since the mortgage payments of do not amortize a zero interest-rate loan; (2) the store of wealth remaining after the house has been paid off, which is relatively high because there are few other savings options; and (3) a portion of the administrative costs of operating the program. Such a program structure must finance current costs either out of future repayments or it must continually contract in size.

Bars IV in Figures 8.1A and 8.1B show the cumulative resource transfers and subsidy levels implied by the higher per-unit subsidy level and the assumed indexation scheme. The net resource transfer (33 100–3 100) is 167 percent of FONAVI expenditures (18 000 australs), and the measured FONAVI net subsidy (18 000–3 100) equals about half of the net transfer received.

The misleading nature of subsidy evaluation using a traditional fiscal accounting concept is particularly striking. Such a traditional measure would suggest that the FONAVI subsidy is equal to 83 percent of its expenditures (18 000 – 3 100)/18 000. The subsidy rate is high but also self-contained, in the sense that revenue collections exceed net expenditures. The 'implosive' nature of the subsidy structure is not apparent. By decomposing the subsidy into its various components, the user-cost perspective helps to show that the program is not self-contained; the repayments do not even cover the costs of administering the program.

8.5   EVALUATING THE EFFICIENCY OF HOUSING SUBSIDIES

FONAVI distributed subsidies in a housing market that does not clear. The conservative estimates in Figure 8.1 suggest that the resource value of a new unit is worth at least 35 percent to 40 percent more than the cost of supplying it. This disequilibrium in the housing market is not the direct result of housing policy. Nevertheless, housing policy is flawed because it does not attempt to reduce the economic losses due to the disequilibrium. Instead, FONAVI distributes very large subsidies with no consideration given to the value of the subsidy. As a result, most of the subsidy is distributed to what can be termed inframarginal households, that is, those households whose behavior is unaffected by the changes in market conditions. It is given to those who already have outstanding loans (through inflation reducing the value of repayments), or those so poor that new housing was unaffordable before the change in macroeconomic conditions.

To get a notion of the efficiency losses implied by this system, consider Figure 8.2. In this figure, the observed stock of housing, q, represents the intersection of the constrained demand-curve for the stock of housing, curve $d'd'$, with the existing stock of housing. This curve is below the demand curve, schedule dd, that could be achieved in a market not in disequilibrium. Suppose further that the FONAVI and BHN subsidies are distributed inframarginally. They shift $d'd'$ to $d''d''$.[17] At the constrained output level, the current value, P_k, exceeds P_o, the long-run equilibrium price. There is no deadweight loss implied by the subsidy's distribution; marginal incentives have not been affected by it. However, the efficiency loss associated with the disequilibrium, area ABC, is also not affected by the subsidy's expenditure.

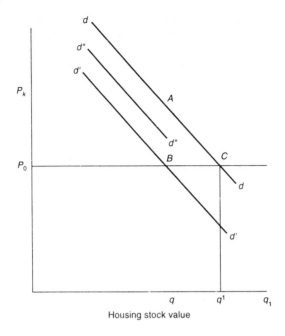

Figure 8.2 Untargeted housing subsidies

A linear approximation of area *ABC* is $1/2(Pk - p_o) \times (q - q_1)$. This figure can be calculated by estimating the difference of *Pk* and *Pc*, applying an estimate of the elasticity of housing demand with respect to this price change times an estimate of the value of the Argentine housing stock. If the housing stock is equal to 100 billion australs, as can be inferred from calculations in Plan Nacional, and the absolute value of the price elasticity is on the order of .75, then the present value of the deadweight loss for Pk/Pc = 1.37 (from the 33 100/24 000 ratio of Figure 8.1) is 4.9 billion australs, or about 6 percent of GDP.[18]

If the subsidies could be directed to those rationed out of the market, they could shift the *d'd'* schedule towards the *dd* curve. Such a shift would reduce the efficiency losses from the sector's disequilibrium. Reducing the per-unit subsidy size from the current levels of more than 15 000 australs per unit to a much smaller lump-sum subsidy, could be expected to induce significant resource mobilization by households. Similarly, reducing the *ex post* subsidies given to those who already own homes could help discriminate between borrowers who are willing to pay for a house and those borrowers who are counting on loan forgiveness to pay for it.

Such a change in approach would allow household savings rather than the government's per-unit transfers to increase as macroeconomic conditions increased the resource value of housing. This is exactly the approach that has been implemented in Chile. In that country, smaller up-front housing subsidies of the order of US $2 500 per unit, and not more than 75 percent of unit cost, were used to leverage household savings. The subsidies there are targeted on those who are willing to mobilize resources of their own, by giving priority to prior household savings in the subsidy distribution criteria (see Castaneda and Quiroz, 1986). With this kind of change in approach, government expenditures should be able to induce more units of housing production per dollar of expenditure. A large increase in production in turn, should lower rents throughout the housing market. Over time, the increase in production could also help to reduce the implicit taxes on household saving. Table 8.1 shows the effects that reductions in these implicit taxes could have on the deadweight losses that occur in the housing market.

The situation described by the right-hand bar in Figure 8.1b is depicted by the middle of the center column of the table. The higher rents and lower after-tax discount rates result in a long-run deadweight loss in Table 8.1 of 4.9 billion australs. The effects of increases in production which lower rent-to-value ratios can be read by going down columns; the effects of reducing the taxes on savings can be read across rows. These figures are meant to be only illustrative. Nevertheless, they show that it is very expensive to focus large per-unit subsidies on the poor rather than on those among the poor who can mobilize resources. They also show that under even slightly less conservative assumptions about the behavior of rents and household discount rates, the present value of the dead-weight losses could be much larger.

Table 8.1 The present value of deadweight losses implied by combinations of housing rent/value ratios and household discount rates (in billions of 1986 australs)

Rent/value	Discount rate		
	.01	.02	.03
.11	8.1	6.2	4.9
.105	7.5	5.7	4.3
.10	6.8	4.9	3.7
.095	6.1	4.3	3.0
.09	5.7	3.8	2.3

8.6 CONCLUSION

A fundamental problem with Argentine housing subsidies is that they are distributed in ways that do not address the disequilibrium in the housing market. As a result, housing production is lower and real rents have risen by more than they would have done, had the subsidies been distributed differently. Another serious problem in the current program is that the level of housing subsidies is determined by inflation or the behavior of real wages, rather than as a policy choice. The per-unit subsidy is not only much larger than the suggested by simple cost figures, it also tends to increase at the 'wrong' times, that is, whenever the inflation rate increases or financial markets tighten. A larger share of the FONAVI transfers essentially provide implicit insurance that protects households from changes in real wages. The reliance on this indirect mechanism to provide real wage insurance is circuitous and inefficient.

The objective of housing policy should be to contain both the direct and prospective effects of housing-market functioning on the rest of the economy. This requires well-defined financial mechanisms, mandating that households share a greater part of inflation or real risks. Such instruments could substantially reduce the government's costs of providing subsidies. Finally, on the subsidy-targeting side, by targeting much smaller subsidies on those lower-income households who can provide evidence that they are closest to the margin, it seems very likely that a much greater number of the more than one million households, who are eligible for FONAVI subsidies, would benefit by a greater aggregate amount.

9 The Fiscal Policy Dimension: Implicit Taxes

9.1 INTRODUCTION

This chapter examines housing policies in socialist economies. While the emphasis is on the Hungarian experience, the questions under investigation also apply to other reforming and post-socialist countries. All the reforming economies are confronted with many of the same basic questions; for example, how can the paradox of a very costly housing-subsidy system be reconciled with the housing shortages that characterize most of the reforming economies; how much do housing subsidies actually cost; and finally, how do housing policies of reformed socialist systems compare with those of market economies?

The two underlying objectives of the chapter are, first, to infer some sense of the overall economic distortions implied by socialist housing policy, and to roughly compare them to market economies; and second, to identify the kinds of empirical data needed to draw firm inferences about policy. Our analysis focuses first on why and how such an internally inefficient system could be developed and maintained. Then we undertake a traditional economic evaluation of this kind of system. Within this framework, the interrelationships between often complicated regulations and their allocative and distributive effects can be analyzed, and some illustrative calculations of the welfare costs of such systems can be made. The analysis shows that the central characteristics of socialist housing policy were: waste of physical and financial resources, and lack of subsidy transparency, causing considerably large welfare costs than in market economies.

The structure of the chapter continues as follows: Section 9.2 discusses housing policy in a socialist system. Section 9.3 provides a historical review of the Hungarian reform experience and its effects on production, ownership, allocation, regulation, and mainte-

nance of the housing stock. Section 9.4 develops a simple framework for examining the welfare costs and transparency of a housing
subsidy and delivery system in what we term classical and reform
socialist systems. Again, while our central emphasis is the Hungarian experience, estimates are also presented for the former Soviet
Union, China, and Poland. Finally Section 9.5 summarizes and identifies areas for future research.

9.2 HOUSING POLICY UNDER SOCIALISM

General Features

In order to understand the rationale for socialist housing policy, the
political conditions prevalent in what we term the first two stages
of socialism – that is, classical and reform socialism need to be
considered. Both stages were characterized by the Communist
Party's monopoly of ideology and power, and by the subordination
of central and local governmental apparatus, to the party. However,
the two periods differ in their approach to economic planning and
management.[1]

Under classical socialism the main regulatory instrument is bureaucratic command; the role of the market accounts only for a very
small share of economic activity. Under reform socialism, the market gains greater influence, although bureaucratic coordination continues to dominate. The post-socialist stage begins with a change of
the political system which evolves into a period of economic transition, in which prices and markets gain an increasingly dominant
role in the allocation and distribution of resources. Free elections
determine the political framework and bring to an end the Communist Party's monopoly on ideology and power. The political reforms
include the creation of a multiparty, parliamentary democracy, and
elected, independent local governments. Limitations on private ownership are reduced or eliminated, and market forces gain ground.

In 1996, the classical socialist system still reigns in Cuba and
North Korea, while economic reforms are going on in China and
Vietnam. Hungary, Poland, and Slovenia acceded to the post-socialist
stage only after several sequences of reforms, while the Czech Republic, Slovakia, East Germany, Bulgaria, Romania, and Albania

skipped to this stage directly from a basically classical phase. The
former Soviet Union represents a hybrid of the above two cases:
deep and far-reaching political reforms have been coupled with halting
economic reform experiments. In essence, however, Russia, and other
republics of the former Soviet Union, have embarked on the post-
socialist road almost directly from the classical system.

Within the classical system, prices and wages are centrally regulated and need to cover only a fraction of the household expenditures
incurred in market economies. For example, wages do not account
for expenditures related to housing, health, education and other essential basic needs and services, which are provided at only a notional cost. As discussed in Chapter 4, to raise the revenues necessary
to provide these services, the state implicitly taxes gross income
and only disburses 'net' wages to its employees. For housing this
implies that incremental production and maintenance of public housing
is determined by planners on the basis of physical targets, estimated
need and available resources. These conditions relegated non-subsidized private initiatives in the housing sector to rural areas, where
investments by the state were limited to developing housing estates
for state-owned farms. Private housing became unaffordable because
access to subsidies was restricted to public housing, whereas the
low national wage and income levels affected everybody. Hence, all
tenants of public rental units received a large implicit subsidy, equal
to the imputed rental value of the unit, less the nominal rental fee
charged[2] regardless of household income or social characteristics.
From a resource allocation perspective, the system operated in a
fundamentally dysfunctional manner.

9.3   THE CASE OF HUNGARY

The Historical Background

The Hungarian experience offers both an opportunity to understand
the shared classical socialist roots and an understanding of the in-
tricacies of reform socialism, which started the country on the path
of post-socialist transition.[3] Hungary has moved a long way from
the classical socialist regime, being the first to introduce an income
tax, a two-tiered banking system, and systematic intergovernmental

relations. Its macroeconomic reforms to stabilize the economy, develop exit procedures for financially troubled enterprises, and change the structure of ownership and production have made the information contained in government budget documents correspond more closely to that of a market economy. Hungary is clearly on its way to becoming a market-based economy.

Housing Policy under the Classical Socialist System

As in most socialist economies, the Hungarian version of 'classical socialism' included the nationalization of the previously private, rental housing stock, whereas owner occupied single-families homes remained in private hands. Contrary to state-owned housing, private ownership precluded access to any state subsidies. Thus, it had to be financed and maintained out of current income and personal savings. Private ownership of real estate, however, was limited to one dwelling or plot per household. The majority of tenants of the nationalized housing stock were allowed to remain in their dwellings, although dislocation occurred to accommodate the requests of households loyal to the new system. Also, authorities assigned co-tenants to many of the larger and better quality apartments. Newly-constructed units belonged to the state and tenants were selected by local councils. Finally, rental rights became *de facto* inheritable properties rights.

Housing conditions in Hungary began to deteriorate under this system. Although the Communist Party and the government both promised improvements to a broad spectrum of society, they could not deliver. Housing ranked far behind the system's more dominant objectives, such as fast-paced growth in industrial output, the strengthening of military power, and independence from the capitalist world market. Individual welfare and consumer sovereignty, and with it housing, did not play an important role in this agenda. Instead, housing policy under 'classical socialism' was founded on the principle that housing was a basic necessity which the state guaranteed its subjects as a citizenship right. This view implied that housing was a benefit in kind, which the state financed through low wages, and which it distributed according to the basic ideological principles of the system.

The premises of socialist policies included discrimination against owner-occupied housing, which did not receive state subsidies.

Although, in principle, market rules and practices prevailed in that segment of the market, they were legally and administratively constrained within narrow bounds. For example, privately-owned housing could be sold or bought legally, but there was no source of finance other than a household's own resources to facilitate such transactions. Nonetheless, even under the classical system, 75 percent of the total housing stock and 40 percent of the urban stock consisted of owner-occupied dwellings. Correspondingly, about 40 percent of urban residents and the vast majority of rural dwellers were deprived of the subsidies given to tenants of public units in the form of capital investments and operating and maintenance costs.

The greatest failure of the 'classical' system's housing policies was that it created the widespread perception of a chronic housing shortage. The damage and partial destruction of the urban housing stock during the war, and forced urbanization following the war, created a real shortage in parts of the country. This would also have occurred in a properly-functioning market economy. The classical socialist system, however, failed to eliminate or reduce perceived and real shortages. Indeed, it deepened them further for the following reasons:

- A marginally growing rental housing supply was confronted with runaway demand unconstrained by household budgets as a consequence of the low rent level. On the other hand, due to the repressed wage level and high construction costs, only a lucky few could afford to built their own homes.
- The bureaucratic allocation of housing reduced mobility and discouraged intercity or interregional moves of individuals, thus contributing to the perception of a real shortage (see Renaud, 1991).
- The state neglected the maintenance and renovation of the housing stock: the condition of housing assets deteriorated markedly, whereas state supply could not keep pace with demand for higher standards.

The distorted price system and the chronic shortage led to the emergence of an extensive black market (see Hegedüs and Tosics, 1988). As part of the post-1968 economic reforms, the Hungarian authorities successfully reintroduced strong incentives for the private sector to invest in housing. Starting in the mid-1970s, Hungary experienced for several consecutive years investment ratios in housing which far exceeded those in the rest of Europe,[4] and in purely statistical terms – that is, the number of dwelling units relative to the number of households – eliminated the physical shortage problem.

Housing Policy under the Reform Socialist System

Under the reform system, market forces gained scope and breadth and revitalized the private-housing sector. The growth of the second economy opened access to additional sources of earnings for a large segment of the population. Part of these earnings were invested in the construction or purchase of a privately-owned home. Financial savings were often supplemented with the household's own physical labor. Hundreds of thousands of houses and condominiums were built through self-exertion.

Initially, the state reacted to this process with benign indifference. It raised neither ideological objections nor legal barriers, instead systematically disregarding breaches of existing administrative restrictions. From the advent of the 1970s, it openly supported the process with cheap land and abetted the home-building effort through low-interest-rate loans, expanding the subsidy system to the private sector as well. In addition, most employers offered a generous leave policy for the construction of an employee's private home. As the reform process deepened, improving the standard of living became a higher priority. This resulted in a boom in private-housing construction. Also, on a small scale, the state began to rehabilitate the inner-city housing stock and to sell a small portion of the public stock to sitting tenants. Rehabilitation and privatization came to a standstill in the mid-1980s. However, the state initiated only small-scale reforms in the public-rental housing sector. Rents were increased marginally in the 1970s and the early 1980s, never exceeding 5 percent of tenants' income.

In assessing the reforms of the past 20 years, we observe the following:

(a) In physical terms, housing conditions improved palpably in relation to the previous period – high investment ratios reduced the housing shortage.

(b) With the improvement of conditions for building private dwell-
    ings, the consumers' range of choices and thus consumer-sov-
    ereignty increased.
(c) In the meantime, to counterbalance the accelerated construction
    cost inflation a large array of subsidies was offered to private,
    owner-occupied housing investment. These subsidies caused sharp
    increases in budgetary expenditures.
(d) The state's own investment in rental housing construction de-
    clined drastically from the early 1980s;
(e) Conditions in the public-rental sector continued to deteriorate
    rapidly as increases in rents fell far behind inflation and as the
    relative share of maintenance subsidies in the state housing-
    budget declined to accommodate the growing demand for sub-
    sidies by the private sector.
(f) Although 'reform socialism' tried to introduce market elements
    into the production and distribution of housing, as we will pres-
    ently show, the costs of the 'reformed socialist housing system'
    remained larger than in market economies.

Major, systematic economic changes began to take hold in the
late 1980s. Macroeconomic stabilization, coupled with fundamental
reforms in trade and enterprise policies opened Hungary's economy
and made the fiscal and resource allocation cost of previous policies more transparent. As labor mobility had increased as a result
of enterprise reform, it also became evident that reform socialism
had failed to increase mobility in the housing sector, and that bu-
reaucracy rather than the market was responsible for responding to
demand and supply. These contradictions contributed to the system's collapse in 1989.

The post-socialist housing policy still had to face the legacy of
the old system. Among the first measures, the central government
delegated the ownership of the public-housing stock and the obliga-
tion to deal with it to the newly established local governments. The
comparative advantage of local government is carrying out this re-
sponsibility is, as shown by Alm and Buckley (1994), highly questionable. Although local governments are politically independent from
the central government and their financial conditions have improved,
they are nevertheless heavily dependent on the central budget. For
public housing, rents have remained far too low and the old main-

tenance subsidies are still being provided, even though they are not identified in the state budget. The measurement of subsidies became even more difficult. The next section presents a simple framework to evaluate the overall efficiency and transparency of the public-housing subsidy system inherited form the socialist system.

Evaluating Public-Housing Subsidies: A Comparative Approach

Even in market economies that have long relied on prices, housing subsidies are difficult to measure in the aggregate, since the demand and supply of housing services are affected by a large number of different, often indirect policies: the income tax code, the structure of the financial system, local regulations, the rate of inflation, and differing social attitudes about the role of the state in distributing resources being among the most important. In addition, in all OECD economies governments also subsidize housing through direct expenditures. Thus, as stressed in Chapter 3, to measure housing subsidies accurately, and the relative efficiency of any housing subsidy delivery system, a comprehensive view of the relative price-effects of various policies must be taken.

For reforming socialist economies, in which housing prices were among the most distorted, these price effects are even more important. In such economies, traditional measures of subsidy are not obvious and readily observable. As shown in the last chapter, measurement involves the complications of inferring the user-cost of capital and comparing it across tenures, of collecting data on rents, prices, and of estimating the elasticities of housing demand and supply. While such measurements have frequently been undertaken in countries with well-developed markets and instruments with which to gauge expectations, they do not necessarily have great precision. But, despite the lack of precision, the clear conclusion of this work is that these effects have significant efficiency and fiscal implications.[5] In countries which have neither relied on markets to allocate resources between sectors or over time, nor used traditional budget documents to identify the government's role in the sector, the precision of cost estimates is even more problematical. One would expect, though, the scale of distortions to be considerably higher, because these countries have had much larger shares of even more mispriced housing capital than market economies.

Greater clarity about the scale of these distortions is needed because the socialist housing system has operated as an interlaced network of indirect and hidden transfers and taxes, as suggested by Table 9.1. In our view, the vast majority of residents in reforming economics are unaware of the fact that their housing expenditures have been implicitly subsidized by the state in one form or another. It also appears that many policy-makers are similarly uninformed about even the broad dimensions of the scale and incidence of the subsidies spent on the housing sector and the regulations which govern its use. This result, after all, should not be surprising, because, as Mayo (1986) has shown, seemingly minor changes in much simpler housing-subsidy program regulations in Germany and the US can result in very large changes in program resource costs.

This chapter does not address the question of whether housing should be subsidized. The focus here is on the inefficiency and the lack of transparency of existing transfers. The traditional measure of the compensated demand, dead-weight loss is used to measure welfare costs.[6] The proportion of the subsidy that appears as a clearly identified expenditure in a government budget is used as a measure of transparency. The greater the ratio, the more transparent is the system.[7]

Now consider how the classical socialist housing-subsidy system fares against the standards identified above. As described in Section 9.2 of this chapter, this system has the following broad characteristics: severe restrictions, if not outright proscriptions, on private transactions with respect to housing; very low nominal rents paid by all occupants of public-rental housing-regardless of income level; administrative allocation of units without regard to the signals that might be inferred from a market; state-controlled production; and through a variety of instruments, an almost total lack of any budgetary recording of the resource costs involved in providing tenants with low-rent housing. This kind of system is almost orthogonal to what has been identified as the components of a well-functioning housing delivery and subsidy system: it provides large per-unit subsidies to all tenants in an economically opaque manner, with little regard to resource costs or budgetary concerns. Furthermore, it effectively sacrifices the central gains afforded by a market: the gains from trade.

Table 9.1   Forms of housing related subsidies in Hungary

	*Open vs hidden** *classical*	*reform* *socialism*	*Targeted vs non-targeted*[b] *classical*	*reform* *socialism*
Low rent public housing	H	H[c]	N	N
Privatized rental dwellings sold at a very low price	–	H	–	N
Bureaucratically allotted cooperative apartments and condos sold at nominal price	H	H	N	N
Bureaucratically alloted land sold at nominal price	–	H	–	N
Construction materials sold at subsidized price	H	O	N	N
Below market level interest rate for private construction	–	O	–	N
Social-welfare allowance	–	O	–	T

Notes: [a] Open transfers are registered in the state budget.
[b] A subsidy is targeted if it is allotted to and received by the entitled (i.e. low-income) families.
[c] The estimated magnitude of the total rental subsidy – World Bank Study – was HUF 33 billion compared to HUF 8.6 billion rental subsidy registered in the state budget.

9.4   AN ANALYSIS OF THE CLASSICAL SOCIALIST SYSTEM: A PARABLE

In a housing delivery system designed primarily to prevent labor from being a commodity – one which relies upon a host of regulatory and administrative controls to allocate services – notions of supply and demand, as discussed in Daniel (1985), are notional rather than strictly empirical. With these difficulties in mind, Figure 9.1 presents what might be termed a parable of the central features of the classical socialist rental-housing market.

The supply of new units as well as maintenance and depreciation are determined by state production decisions, so that the supply curve of public-housing services, *QS*, is vertical at a level selected by the state. Assume, for the moment, that this level of supply is the amount of public-housing services that would be demanded in a market

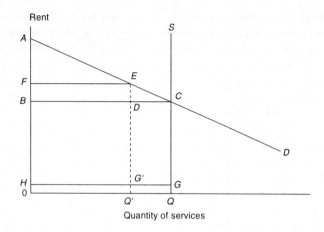

Figure 9.1   Classical socialism

economy. This assumption implies an equilibrium so that the return
of housing services equals that of alternative investments. In this
case, the resource price of the flow of housing services would be
OB. Notional demand, as Daniel (1989) and Alexeev (1988) have
shown, appears to follow similar patterns to those of market economies, and is depicted by curve *AD*. Rents are set at a very low
level, *OH*, and a portion of the 'tax' revenue imposed on all wage
earners finances these rents. With our assumption that the equilibrium resource-cost of housing services is equal to *OB*, the amount
of the rent reduction is area *HBCG*. In addition to the controls on
incremental output, which create a vertical supply curve, severe restrictions also exist on exchanging the housing allocated by the state
(as described for China by Tolley, 1991). In the classical system,
because of the inability to trade, the area *ABC* is effectively un-
obtainable. For a first approximation, the efficiency cost would equal
this triangle.

Of course, the assumption that *OQ* supply of public housing is
the amount that would be supplied by a market economy is a strong
one, particularly in light of the lack of feedback mechanisms that
prevent planners from responding to conditions of excess demand
or supply. In fact, if we follow the discussions in Andrusz (1990),
Szelenyi and Conrad (1983), or Kornai (1986) with respect to the

former Soviet Union and Hungary, particularly up through the 1960s, it would appear that the *ex ante* output level selected by the classical system was significantly less than the equilibrium level of output OQ. The urban public-housing stock ranges from about 40 percent of the housing stock in Hungary to over 70 percent in Russia and China. Similarly, if the very low levels of chinese housing investment, as a share of GDP over the 1949 to 1978 period – 1.5 percent – are compared to housing GDP investment patterns in other countries at similar levels of development – on the order of 3 percent – it would appear that China's pre-1979 output levels were to the left of OQ by a considerable amount, such as the amount described by OQ'.[8]

'In the case where output is constrained below the steady-state demand for housing, that is, OQ', the welfare loss due to the inability to trade is reduced to area AFE. Area $FEDB$ is redistributed from the state and non-beneficiaries to tenants of public housing in a manner that, according to Alexeev (1988) and Daniel (1985), has been regressive.[9] However, because policy has shifted the supply curve to the left by QQ' and another sector's or sectors' supply curve(s) to the right by a corresponding amount, the area to the right of $Q'E$ is also lost to consumers, as planners underinvested in the housing stock. The rectangle $DCGG'$ has been redistributed, like area $FEDB$, to other sectors, less a welfare loss associated with any non-lump sum redistribution method. Hence, under a constrained system the welfare loss is reduced to areas $AFE + EDC + \lambda$ where λ represents the efficiency losses associated with redistributing $DCGG'$ to other sectors. If $\lambda < FEDB$, our welfare loss estimates, based on a equilibrium level of public housing stock, that is area ABC, will be overstated.

Interpreting time-series data on housing investment in one socialist economy, much less comparing such investments across countries, is a practice fraught with methodological difficulties, as discussed for example in Prell (1989). The approach we have chosen is to use Goldsmith's (1985) careful study of comparative national balance-sheets for the two socialist economies which he examined, the former Soviet Union and Hungary, and then attempt to replicate this kind of estimate of the value of the housing stock for China and Poland. Our replications rely upon World Bank country studies and Kingsley and Struyk (1992), and modifications described in an appendix.

Like Laidler (1969), Rosen (1979), and Hills (1991), we assume
that public housing, *VPH*, yields a gross real rate of return to housing, *GR*. At the steady-state output level, the housing stock would
earn a return sufficient to cover the costs of maintenance and depreciation, yielding a gross real return on the order of 6.5 percent.[10]
Multiplication of *GR* by *VPH/Y* where *Y* is GDP yields *R*, a measure
of the flow of gross rental services as a fraction of GDP. This figure
is presented in the right hand column of Table 9.2.

Using figures on rent-to-income payments from market economies
we can then estimate how much of this yield derives from household payments and how much is a transfer. For example, because
market rents in market economies equal about 25 percent of income, a rent-to-income figure of 5 percent implies a subsidy-rate of
80 percent of the gross rate of return. In addition, because households in socialist economies have paid rents below the cost of maintenance, this 80 percent figure exceeds total net return; besides this
amount, these households have also received a subsidy equal to any
allowances for depreciation expenses, as well as some portion of
the maintenance expenses. Thus, the subsidy tenants receive, that
is, area *BCGH*, is equal to .065 less the portion of this gross return
paid to tenants. These figures are presented in Table 9.3 which shows
an annual subsidy-level ranging from almost 3.2 percent of GDP
for the former Soviet Union to between 1 and 2 percent of GDP in
Hungary and Poland.

Our loss estimates and the size of the loss relative to the size of
the transfer – on the order of 50 percent – are large. The former
compares, for example, with estimates of loss of about $\frac{1}{2}$ percent
of GDP as estimated for home-ownership subsidies by Hendershott
and Hu (1980) and as can be inferred from Rosen (1979); and the
latter with the less than 25 percent of the rental housing subsidy for
Germany, as estimated by Mayo (1986). Accordingly, even if systematic underinvestment in housing reduces our estimates, the costs
in the former Soviet Union and China are still more than twice the
largest estimate for the US's largest housing subsidy. Welfare costs
in Hungary and Poland are equal to the largest estimate for the US,
and their size relative to the size of the subsidy given is twice the
German level. Clearly the classical socialist system was a highly
inefficient way of delivering housing services.[11]

While the graphical analysis is simple, it also helps to clarify

Table 9.2   Urban public-housing services as a share of GDP (1988)

	Capital/GDP	Public-housing/ capital	Public-housing/GDP	Public-housing Income as a share of GDP (%)
Russia/USSR	4.80	.11	.52	3.4
Hungary	5.55	.06	.33	2.1
China	5.39	.08	.43	2.8
Poland	5.17	.05	.26	1.7

Sources: See appendix to this chapter.

Table 9.3   Housing subsidy cost and transparency[12]

	Public-housing subsidy as a share of GDP	Generalized welfare loss as a share of GDP		Government expenditures as a share of transfers
	(%)	A	B	(%)
Russia/USSR	3.2	1.60	1.12	16.0
Hungary	1.7	0.85	0.60	1.6
China	2.7	1.35	0.95	15.8
Poland	1.4	0.70	0.49	6.3

Sources: See appendix to this chapter.

sources of differences because it shows that only two factors matter in determining the size of the subsidy: (1) the share of the housing stock to which it applies, OQ, and (2) the level of the rent subsidy $OB - OH$. The much larger Russian subsidy occurs mostly because the Russian urban public-housing stock is three times the share of the Hungarian one. In addition, the subsidy-rate is larger. However, at the very low rent levels prevailing in all the socialist countries, even with a fourfold increase in rent – the amount by which the Hungarian rent-to-income ration exceeded the Russian figure before Russia's recent extremely high levels of inflation – there is little reduction in efficiency-loss due to higher rents. Surprisingly, however, there is a large reduction in subsidy-transparency presented by traditional budget measures.

The latter result occurs because of the effect that a change in rents has on the ratio of budgeted transfers, T, to unbudgeted transfers, S. The numerator in the ratio is the amount of the transfers that appear in the government's budget documents, a figure equal to $m - \beta RT$, where m is annual maintenance expense, RT is the rent payments by households, and β is the same share of maintenance expenses covered by rents. For all reforming economies $0 < \beta < 1$, that is, rents do not cover maintenance expenditures. The denominator, S, is equal to $i + d + (m - \beta RT)$, where i is the net real return, and d is depreciation expenses. From this arrangement $d(T/S)/dRT < 0$ as long as $\beta RT < m$. That is, as long as rents are lower than maintenance costs, and the methods of accounting for housing subsidies in government budgets measure only this difference, higher rents only reduce the small amount of the total transfer accounted for by government expenditures; they have a smaller effect on total transfers.

In the Hungarian case, rents almost cover maintenance expenditures, and government expenditures account for less than 2 percent of total transfers. In the Russian case, in contrast, household expenditures cover very little of these maintenance expenses. As a result, in the Hungarian case the subsidies measured in the budget are almost invisible, almost all of the transfer is 'off the books'. In the Russian case the size of the discrepancy between measured and actual transfers is large (the latter is 6 times larger). But the discrepancy across countries is even larger, with budgeted expenditures equalling 15.9 percent of transfers in Russia *vs* only 1.5 percent of transfers measured in Hungary. Accordingly, the 1992 Hungarian policy of eliminating the budgeted rental subsidies carries with it little of the budget austerity one might associate with a budget cut which eliminated housing expenditures for maintenance. It eliminated only 1.5 percent of the transfers.

The Analytics of the Reform System

The changes implied by reform socialism are characterized in Figure 9.2. The first change to consider is to the elasticity of the supply curve of housing services. Instead of a vertical supply curve, under reform socialism there is some supply responsiveness to prices. That responsiveness, however, is largely technologically determined, with the degree of responsiveness dictated by the malleability and location of the existing housing stock, and the marketability of housing as an asset. The housing stock's physical characteristics constrain the rate at which it can be subdivided, and the rate at which structure can be substituted for land. If most of the public units are physically small, it will be difficult to subdivide units in response to higher demand for a unit in a particular location. Similarly, if units are located – as Bertaud and Renaud (1995) have shown they are in Moscow and Warsaw – in cities in which the urban population-density function increases rather than falls with distance from the city center, then the supply elasticity of housing service will necessarily be lower than that provided by a housing stock that was built with a density that responded to market incentives. In many of the larger cities of reforming economies, single-family low-density flats in the central city will have to be replaced by different arrangements of land and structure inputs. Conversely, the present relatively high-density living units at the urban periphery will be in considerably lower demand, particularly if the extremely underpriced urban transport systems increase fares. In such places supply will be considerably less elastic than the estimates made for market economies.

In the reform socialism case, curve QS in Figure 9.1 becomes OS in Figure 9.2 at the resource cost of housing and O^1S^1 after subsidies. If there were no restrictions on transfers in the reform system, the new market equilibrium would be at point Z, where AD intersects O^1S^1, and the efficiency losses would be reduced as long as $GCZ < ABC$. That is, the system would be less inefficient as long as the losses involved with providing large housing subsidies to a responsive market would be balanced against the gains from allowing exchanges to occur (area ABC). In a frictionless market, the latter would be eliminated, and with an estimate of supply elasticity the size of GCZ could be calculated to determine the welfare costs of the reform system. However, even in the reform system, restrictions on and ambiguities about transfers remain: the marketability of public housing is severely constrained.[13] Swaps of units with side payments and illegal sublettings characterize most transactions with the result that there is a 50 percent discount on the exchange of units in public housing relative to what the unit would command on the private market (Daniel and Semjen, 1987).

This discount can be viewed as the size of the marketability premium, or the size of a bid – ask spread that applies to housing

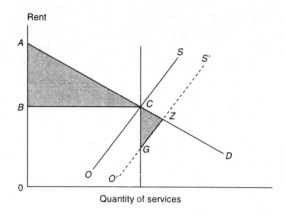

Figure 9.2   Reform socialism

transactions.[14] The result is that both the supply and demand curves per unit of time are to the left of the long-run equilibrium schedules. Of course, a significant portion of these marketability premia are what might be termed policy-induced, in that they are the result of the operating legal framework. In this respect, they are similar to a tax wedge – a wedge which reduces the welfare gains associated with eliminating the prohibition on exchange.

In summary, we cannot directly answer questions of what is the cost and transparency of the reforming socialist system without information on a wide range of country- and even city-wide idiosyncratic factors such as: (1) the elasticity of supply of services, with its dependencies on the structure and location of the existing stock; (2) the effect that legal prohibitions or ambiguities have on the real estate marketability premium; and (3) the amount of tax avoidance available through non-socialist earnings. This last effect would shift the demand curve to the right.

We can, nevertheless, draw the following conclusions. First, from an economic perspective, transparency is not improved relative to the opaqueness that characterizes the classical system. Indeed, it may even deteriorate, as our example in Table 9.3 suggests. Essentially, it is impossible to say how much is transferred and to whom it is given. Second, while the costs of subsidy delivery in the reform system are lower than they are in the classical system, they are almost certainly considerably higher than those in market economies, either in terms of the share of GDP or as a portion of the transfer made. This result occurs because the costs associated with the prohibitions on trade have been essentially replaced by the costs of: (1) permitting trade of the low-rent tenancies; and (2) not permitting enforcement of contracts. Instead of well-targeted subsidies to those thought to be deserving of assistance, large per-unit subsidies are still provided to a larger share of the population, regardless of the tenants' income level. The ability to exchange *de facto* property rights remains limited. It is, in short, a case of replacing one inefficient delivery mechanism with another. Ultimately, until contracts are made enforceable and subsidies more transparent, the reforms will fail. To improve efficiency, efforts to change the housing allocation system must address the irrationality of the 'game' that was used as an alternative to a market system. Ignoring the cost of existing property rights while simultaneously impeding, but not restricting their transfer, does not change this system.

9.5 CONCLUSION

The socialist system was designed to subordinate the plans of individuals to the plans of the state. Perhaps nowhere was this subordination clearer than in the case of housing, a good which permits one of the most obvious manifestations of personal and bourgeois tastes. It follows that the housing delivery mechanism developed by the socialist system attempted to constrain the development of markets for housing services. It also follows that a market-oriented analysis of this sort of system, such as this chapter, would necessarily find the system wanting. Just how wanting, however, has never been previously estimated.

Our analysis presents the first attempt to estimate the aggregate cost of the socialist rental housing system. While we recognize that our estimates are imprecise, the cost is no doubt very large, and multiplicatively larger than the highest estimates for market economies. Our analysis also indicates that increased economic transparency, and hence the accountability for these transfers probably declines as the systems reform. Finally, we suggest the following important areas where further work is needed: (1) empirical analysis is required if useful summary statistics about sector performance are to be made; and (2) priorities for policy analysis should include improving subsidy targeting and reducing marketability premia.

9.6 APPENDIX

The construction of Tables 9.4 and 9.5 required making estimates of the capital stock, the gross rate of return (GRR), and the subsidy rate. These computations required: (1) gathering and in some cases interpolating data which was as comparable as possible for the four countries, and (2) estimating the annual housing subsidy rate. As recent studies show, many basic data are simply unavailable. For an aggregate analysis of a long lived good such as housing that has been systematically mispriced and undermaintained for many years, considerable caution is warranted.

Housing Stock Data

Table 9.5 uses measures of the urban housing stock (UH) to derive the annual flow of housing services as described in the text. Table 9.4 shows the intermediate steps used in moving from one column to the next in Table 9.5. Column 1 in Tables 9.5 and 9.4 is a measure of capital – output (K/O). This data are from Goldsmith (1985) or World Bank Country Economic Memoranda for the respective countries. The data for Russia on capital – output are consistent with those reported by Easterly and Fischer (1993). The measure of capital is tangible assets excluding gold and silver. Output is GDP. Where possible, data from Goldsmith (1985) are used in the construction. His work provides the best available comparative data for two of the countries in the table (Hungary and Russia [USSR]). For the estimate of Poland's capital output, and housing-capital ratios figures, data from Hungary and the Soviet Union were averaged. For K/O this approach was taken because it was much more conservative than the World Bank Country estimate of 7.0 for the more narrow fixed capital-output ratio. For H/K the average was used because no alternative data was available.

Updating the Hungarian and the Russian figures for the percent of housing investment in total investment outlays which were 18.9 and 14.7 respectively, and adjusting for housing's longer asset life results in insignificant changes in H/K. For investment figures see Matras (1989).

For China, balance sheet data is not available. To attempt to account for the effects of its much lower *per capita* income and lower share of urban population (in comparison with the other reform economies mentioned), India's ratios, for H/K, for which data exist, were used. Again, the source is Goldsmith. For China's K/O ratio the World Bank capital – output figure was used. Column 2 in Table 9.4 is an estimate of the value of urban housing. Urban Population as a percentage of Total Population (World Bank, 1992b) is used to approximate the share of Urban Housing in Total Housing (UH/H). This aggregation is somewhat arbitrarily, but we think conservatively, assumes that the greater amount of rural housing space is offset by higher urban land values. Column 3 in Table 9.4 is the share of residential structure in reproducible assets less consumer durables and livestock. The latter accounted for slightly more than 1 percent of reproducible assets and so has little effect on the estimates. It was deleted from the non-residential capital stock as being a non-durable consumer good. Similarly, consumer durables were deleted because they are often embodied in real-estate value or even more price-distorted consumption goods. The share of the urban housing stock that is publicly-owned (PH/UH) is taken from World Bank studies. All but the Hungarian data are inclusive of employer-owned housing (World Bank 1991b, 1992a). Column (5) in Table 9.4 is equal to the product of columns (1) through (4).

Annualized Flow Figures

In the spirit of the literature as in, for example, Laidler (1969), Rosen (1979) and Poterba (1992), the gross rental value is assumed to be 6.5 percent. This is a somewhat conservative estimate relative to Laidler's 7.5 percent, and Poterba's 10.5 percent. Multiplying UPH/O by this gross return yields housing income as a share of GDP (HY/O), column 6.

Annual Housing Subsidy

Table 9.3 converts the income from the housing stock into a subsidy level as a share of GDP. It identifies the share of budgeted expenditures relative to transfers. The estimate of the subsidy starts with the assumption that the observed unsubsidized rent-to-income ratios paid in market economies yield a 6.5 percent gross rate of return. Evidence from the World Bank Housing Indicators Program (Mayo and Angel, 1992), suggests that renters pay at least 25 percent of income for gross rent in market economies. In socialist economies, the highest average rent-to-income level was 4.5 percent in Hungary (Kingsley and Maxiam, 1992); whereas in China and Russia it is closer to one percent (World Bank, 1992a). If the 25 percent of income used for market rent yields a gross rate of return (GRR) of 6.5 percent, then dividing the R/Y figures in socialist economies by 25 percent provides a measure of the share of the GRR paid by households. In this cases $1-[(R/Y)/.25]$ gives a measure of the share of the GRR that the government provides. The subsidy rate as a share of output is then determined: $S/O = HY/O * 1 - (R/Y).25$.

Table 9.4 Income from stock housing

	(1) K/O	(2) UH/H	(3) H/K	(4) PH/UPH	(5) UPH/O	(6) HY/O (%)
Russia/USSR	4.80	.74	.18	.83	0.52	3.4
Hungary	5.55	.61	.21	.50	0.33	2.1
China	5.39	.56	.19	.80	0.43	2.8
Poland	5.17	.62	.20	.40	0.26	1.7

Notes: *K/O*: Capital – output ratio Broad capital – output ratio source: Goldsmith (1985, Table 16) and World Bank (1983b).

UH/H: Urban housing as a share of total housing. *Source*: World Bank (1992a).

H/K: Residential structures as a share of reproducible tangible assets less consumer durables and livestock. Source: Goldsmith (1985, Appendix A, Tables A8, A9, A16).

PH/UH: Public housing as a share of urban housing, State housing stock ownership. *Source*: World Bank (1992a, 1991a, 1991b, 1991c).

UPH/O: Urban public housing as a share of GDP. *UPH/O = K/O* PH/K*.

HY/O: Housing income as a share of GDP. *HY/O = UPH/O* .065*.

The Budgeted Subsidy

The measure of the subsidy differs from government housing subsidy expenditures because in every case the share of the GRR paid by households was less than the amount needed to cover maintenance costs, and government expenditures only cover the difference between these expenses and rents.

Loss Estimates

In calculating the welfare costs or Generalized Deadweight Loss (GDL), we relied on a simple measure of it as defined by Poterba (1992) and Rosen (1979). The elasticity which determines the deadweight loss is given by $\varepsilon = \eta + w\sigma$, where w is the good's budget share, h is the price elasticity, and s is the income elasticity. Consensus estimates of h equal to about 21.0 or 21.5 in market economies are used, as in Poterba (1992) or White and White (1977). For income elasticities a number of complications arise. The first issue is whether σ is elastic or inelastic. From Malpezzi and Mayo (1987a), we know that income elasticities in developing nations are inelastic contemporaneously, but elastic as income levels grow. Because the form of compensation is equivalent to increasing income, the elastic figure seems the appropriate one. However, which level of w is appropriate in a reforming economy? To account for these effects, as well as the possible sup-

Table 9.5   Transfers and subsidies in selected countries

	R/Y	S/O (%)	GDL_A	GDL_B	T/S (%)
Russia/USSR	0.01	3.2	1.60	1.120	16.0
Hungary	0.045	1.7	0.85	0.595	1.6
China	0.01	2.7	1.35	0.945	15.8
Poland	0.035	1.4	0.70	0.490	6.3

S/O: Subsidy level as a share of GDP: $S/O = HY/O* \left[1 - \frac{(R/Y)}{.25} \right]$.

GDL: Generalized dead weight loss: $GDL_A = S/O* \ 0.5$, $GDL_B = GDL_A* \ 0.7$.

T/S: Expenditures as a share of transfers.

Note: R/Y: Rent level as a share of income.
Source: Kingsley and Struyk (1992) and World Bank (1992b).

pression of housing investments to below an equilibrium level, we present two measures: one, $\varepsilon = -1.0$, and the other, $\varepsilon = -.7$.

Expenditures as a share of transfers, T/S, is the ratio of government expenditures to the measure of the subsidy level. Once again, budgeted government expenditures are equal to the costs of maintenance less rents received from tenants. Depreciation is not budgeted. T/S was computed from the following equation:

$$T/S = \frac{[.0125 - .065 * \frac{R/Y}{.25}] \ UPH}{S}$$

10 The Real Sector Dimension: Constraints on Encouraging the Private Sector

10.1 INTRODUCTION

This chapter shows how the new National Housing Policy (NHP) adopted in Nigeria in 1992 can be considered within the framework of analysis presented in the first section of this book. In particular, it evaluates the new proposal for the private sector and shows how this proposal attempts to link the housing and financial markets. The language of the new policy approach promotes the private sector as the chief means to address the severe shortages and costs of shelter in Nigeria. However, it appears that many of the key measures advocated could be counterproductive to both private-sector development and the Structural Adjustment Program (SAP). Through a review of the strategies and programs that other countries have used to rejuvenate their shelter sector, this chapter provides information on how the NHP might be revised to better exploit the private sector, operate more efficiently and sustainably, and contribute to, rather than impede, the Structural Adjustment Program.

For the past decade, the average level of GDP invested in housing in Nigeria has been declining. In addition, imported materials continue to account for a large portion of the inputs used in housing construction, and mortgage finance has become increasingly scarce and unaffordable. In an effort to reform the housing sector, the Nigerian government recently adopted a new strategy under which the government is to act as 'an enabler, promoter and facilitator conducive to individual and co-operative housing efforts'. This new approach could serve to make the housing sector more productive and contribute to increased domestic production of housing inputs. How-

146

ever, the financial instruments proposed to fulfill these objectives are not conducive to these ends and may well produce the opposite effect: increasing the role of the public sector, and expanding the distortions that have undermined the functioning of the housing market.

The main instruments of the NHP are (1) a new wage tax to finance housing, similar to that described in Chapter 8's discussion of Argentina; (2) increased directed credit for housing at low interest rates, and increased competition for deposit resources from newly created and undercapitalized mortgage institutions, and (3) increased access to subsidized credit for public-sector housing producers. A newly created National Housing Fund will finance the sector through the Federal Mortgage Bank of Nigeria (FMBN), which will then on-lend to newly created private-sector institutions. The National Housing Fund will operate through three mechanisms. First, a mandatory 2.5 percent tax on all wage earners earning more than N3000 (about US$ 150) per year; these contributions would be put into a retirement fund with a low nominal yield that is currently about negative 25 percent. Second, contributions equalling 10 percent of loanable funds from all commercial and merchant banks; they would earn an interest rate 1 percent higher than the rate chargeable on current account deposits, thereby reducing profitability of these banks. Third, investments of 10 percent of non-life funds and 20 percent of life funds of insurance companies; these funds will be invested at a 4 percent nominal interest rate which will result in substantial losses for the insurance industry at the current level of inflation – in excess of 20 percent.

Alternatives to the forced savings scheme proposed in the NHP are available and currently under implementation in other countries, such as Ghana, Mexico, and Poland. In addition, as described by Diamond and Lea (1992), European countries that have long favored savings for housing schemes are reducing their support for such earmarked savings systems. Finally, as discussed in Chapter 6, there are alternatives to the credit subsidies implied by low nominal-rate mortgage loans. Indexed mortgages, for instance, may be an alternative. Such a mechanism has worked effectively in nearby Ghana.

10.2 THE ROLE OF THE PRIVATE SECTOR IN NIGERIAN HOUSING

Private-sector development in the Nigerian shelter sector has been at a standstill for more than a decade. With few exceptions, the private-sector transactions that have taken place have been informal and on the fringe of legality. At the opposite end of the spectrum, public-sector activity is plagued with many problems. Instead of operating as a social policy, it operates more like a regressive lottery or patronage system. The results have been the simultaneous construction of some of the most luxurious subsidized housing in Africa, and general deterioration in the housing conditions of most Nigerians, particularly the housing conditions of the poor. The changes proposed in the new NHP could well expand the public-sector role in those areas where private sector development could make the greatest contribution – the financing and production of housing.

Over the four years of the SAP, ending in 1990, the average level of investment in housing was 1.7 percent of GDP. This figure is almost half the 3.3 percent share achieved in the preceding decade, and this share has secularly declined from over 3.6 percent of GDP in 1975 to 1.5 percent in 1990.[1] The adjustment process is clearly related to a reduction in the amount invested in housing. However, this period also witnessed an oscillation and a decline in oil prices and correspondingly national income. Such macroeconomic trends would also have negative effects on long-term investments such as housing. Hence, the exact cause of the secular decline in housing investment over the past 15 years is impossible to identify. But, what is clear is that the full cost of new housing, as produced in Nigeria, is reflected increasingly in the prices paid. For example, a conservative estimate of the foreign exchange content of housing investment in 1990 was such that the price of imported materials for housing construction was greater than income from all non-oil exports.

With the depreciation of the naira, the national unit of currency, the full cost of housing constructed primarily from imported materials (on the order of 50 to 60 percent of inputs) becomes clearer.[2] For instance, consider the case of a family who in 1986 purchased a new home, constructed from 50 percent imported materials. Suppose, conservatively, that the structure accounted for 70 percent of the cost of the house, and that the cost of the house was five times annual income.[3] If that family were to buy the same house with the same imported materials in 1991, because of the reduced value of the naira the house would require more than twelve times annual income. If the further reductions in the naira's value over 1992 are taken into account, these cost increases become even more pronounced. In this kind of price environment, the surprise is not that import-based housing investment declined, but that the decline was not greater.

As the preceding example shows, domestic input markets have failed to replace the imported materials used in housing construction. One reason for this failure is doubt that a complete adjustment has occurred in the foreign exchange market. Until March of 1992, a parallel market for foreign exchange existed, with premia averaging over 30 percent. Hence, even though the official value of the naira had fallen, for domestic producers there was a reasonable expectation of the need for further substantial reductions. Such a prospect does not provide a credible basis for domestic producers to begin a serious investment program in an industry that produces non-tradable goods. The result is a lack of private-sector interest in developing the input industry, even though significant, but not complete adjustment had taken place.[4] A credible foreign exchange market is essential for encouraging private investment in the housing sector.

For the encouragement of private-sector input production, the most important step is the development of a credible macro- and sectoral environment. This credibility will have much more important effects than increased funding for research into low-cost housing production techniques and manpower training programs as recommended in the NHP. Of course, attention should be given to making sure that building approval standards are not inhospitable to the development of more reliance on locally produced goods. But, the keys to credibility on a macro level are two: (1) a freely determined exchange rate, so that imports are not subsidized relative to domestic production, and (2) a less inflationary environment so that long-term finance can prosper.

On a sectoral level, credibility requires access to land and finance on competitive, affordable terms, and the allocation of domestic input production on a market rather than administrative basis. if this kind of credible environment can be put in place, then an important complementary policy change could make the NHP consistent rather than competitive with the SAP. This policy could substitute the expansion of finance for the currently proposed expansion of government transfers and contingent liabilities.[5]

10.3 HOUSING-FINANCE POLICY UNDER THE NHP

The part of the new NHP that has received the greatest amount of public attention and which the policy document refers to as the centerpiece of the new approach is the establishment of a National Housing Fund which will finance the sector through the Federal Mortgage Bank of Nigeria (FMBN). The FMBN which is a designated APEX, or centralized, lending institution will on-lend to newly created private sector mortgage institutions.

Capital for the National Housing Fund will be raised through three main sources:

1. A mandatory 2.5 percent tax on all wage-earners earning N3000 (about US$150) or more per year. These contributors would be able to withdraw these funds at retirement, with a low nominal yield that is currently about *negative 25 percent*. Families saving at this real after-inflation rate of interest will have serious problems. For instance, in ten years their current contributions will be worth about 10 kobo (that is, 10 percent) on each naira of contribution. And, if inflation increases, contributions will continue to devalue.

2. All commercial and merchant banks would contribute 10 percent of their loanable funds in this Fund at the FMBN. They would earn an interest rate 1 percent higher than the rate (currently a maximum of 5 percent) chargeable on current account deposits. Hence, this measure would imply that commercial bank profitability would be reduced by the difference in the rate they would have earned on their current undirected loans that would in the future have to be put in the housing fund. In the spring of 1992, the interest on inter-bank loans was on the order of 45 percent. The difference is thus a reduction in return of about 40 percent, and because this lower return applies to 10 percent of bank lending it would in turn result in an average return on total lending that was lower by about four percent. To maintain their current level

of profitability, banks would have to increase their spread by 3 to 4 percent. Hence, even ignoring commercial bank problems with bad loans and the Central Bank's estimate that about one-third of the country banks are 'unhealthy' or 'distressed',[6] this policy is not consistent with a well-functioning banking system. For merchant banks, the implied tax rate could be even higher because their return on unrestricted lending is higher. They can, however, avoid at least some of the tax by changing the mix of their investments away from lending.

3. Insurance companies would be required to invest 10 percent of their non-life funds and 20 percent of their life funds in real estate with at least half of these amounts going to the housing fund at a four percent nominal interest rate. Once again the losses would be substantial at an estimated N52.7 million annually.[7] Unless inflation were to fall quickly and permanently, these investments in the National Housing Fund would not be sustainable.

In addition, the federal government has released a N250 million take-off grant to ensure the viability of the Fund.[8]

The FMBN will lend the proceeds to newly established primary lenders, called mortgage institutions. As of August 1992, 61 such institutions had been licensed with an extremely low capital requirement of five million naira (about US$220 000), and over 200 other firms were seeking such licenses. The plan is for the mortgage institutions to on-lend the proceeds to individual borrowers, with 80 to 85 percent financing from the National Housing Fund while these mortgage institutions will mobilize the residual portion of the loan, earning a 4 percent spread on their cost of borrowing from FMBN. Earning this 4 percent spread on 80 percent of the loan would permit these new institutions to compete aggressively for deposits. Hence, other deposit based lenders, such as banks, would be confronted on both sides of their balance sheets: more competition for deposits from new institutions and more constraints on earnings from the lower interest rates on their earmarked assets.

Perhaps the most striking deficiency of the National Housing Fund is that it fails to benefit its target population – families of modest income – due to fundamental loopholes in the plan. Workers earning at least N3000 per year contribute to the Fund and are its expected beneficiaries. The Fund authorizes N80 000 as the minimum amount of a loan and 25 years as the maximum lending period. At the current rates of interest, N3200 is the minimal yearly mortgage payment under these conditions. This amount is higher than the annual salary of many contributors, and when the interest rate is considered, the disparity between the borrower's annual income and the expected mortgage payment is more acute.[9]

Other details of the fund's operation are designed to ensure that it operates equitably, such as preferences for lower-income families, and (perhaps) limits on the loan amounts. But rather than focus on the problems with these details, it is important to clearly identify the main problem with this approach: severe financial sector problems are a likely result. Using (1) thinly capitalized, new institutions in (2) an inflationary environment to on-lend funds that (3) are mobilized through tax and regulatory coercion for (4) a sector that has significant collection problems will not work. The likelihood of very costly failure is almost certain. The possibility that this financial scheme will contribute to private-sector development is highly doubtful.

10.4 HOUSING-FINANCE POLICY IN OTHER COUNTRIES

Other countries have had little success in implementing housing-finance schemes through strictly public-sector institutions such as the FMBN. There is no obvious reason why institutions of this sort should be wholly publically owned. Nor is there a rationale for operations to be outside the purview of financial-sector regulations, as is currently the situation with the FMBN. The reliance on public-sector institutions to finance the sale and construction of housing has proved to be extremely problematic and ultimately inefficient in other nations. Often such arrangements increase stagnation of the housing sector. Ghana provides an instructive example.

The housing sector in Ghana has many characteristics in common with that of Nigeria. The Ghanaian shelter sector has been characterized by a high cost-to-income ratio, low housing quality, housing parastatals that are barely functional. It also has a bankrupt domestic-inputs market, a financial environment of high inflation, low, unindexed nominal interest rates, and extensive direction of credit to unsuccessful parastatals. For the past three decades, two parastatal organizations, the State Housing Corporation (SHC) and the Tema Development Corporation (TDC), were the primary sources of housing production. The Bank for Housing and Construction provided mortgage finance. All are public-sector organizations. Both the SHC and TDC have operated in deficit for several years, surviving by government subsidies. These public-sector organizations have been ineffective in fostering the development of the housing and construction industry. As a result, the production of housing through these agencies dwindled to only a few hundred units per year.

A World Bank Urban project in Ghana was designed to begin counteracting these problems, mainly through restructuring the housing production industry and housing finance system. The project also provided technical assistance to perform detailed financial and institutional studies on the housing parastatals for developing a plan to reform and restructure the agencies.

In Nigeria, as in other countries, the reliance on a large number of new private-sector institutions with little or no nominal capital requirements is extremely risky under the best of circumstances. Usually the capital requirements for private-sector mortgage institutions are at least four or five times higher than those authorized under the NHP. In other countries, such insufficient capital requirements have resulted in the government having to subsidize or 'bail out' the private-sector institution.

The ongoing US Savings and Loan (S&L) crisis provides an example of the possible detrimental effects of undercapitalized firms operating in the financial sector. The S&L crisis can be traced back to policy decisions during the early 1980s that permitted the S&Ls' capital to erode from a level considerably higher than those mandated by the NHP.[10] Traditionally, S&Ls lent funds on 20–30 year mortgages at fixed rates of interest and funded themselves through short-term deposits, a structure very similar to that proposed for Nigeria's new lenders. During the late 1970s and early 1980s, higher inflation rates and correspondingly the higher interest rates that the S&Ls had to pay depositors, sharply decreased earnings, eroding capital. At the same time that capital was eroded by increases in interest rates, financial deregulation phased out interest-rate ceilings on deposits, allowed new lending practices, and increased the maximum size of insured deposits from US$40 000 to US$100 000.

This new regulatory regime provided greater freedom of investment. And, since the S&Ls were required to risk little of their own
capital, any losses beyond the low levels of capital in the firms
were absorbed by the US government. While this type of structure
ensured the plentiful supply of mortgage credit and competitive mortgage lenders, it also induced much risk-taking by the S&Ls, risk-
taking with capital they did not have. This risk-taking resulted in
bankruptcy for many S&Ls; in the end the US government will pay
in excess of $200 billion so that the Savings and Loan Associations
can meet their obligations.

The use of ear-marked taxes to mobilize funds for low cost mortgage credit, as has been proposed in the NHP, is problematic in an
inflationary environment. As an alternative to this forced savings
scheme, which expropriates savings, savings could be invested in
indexed mortgages rather than in negative-return government securities that, for example, the National Provident Fund (NPF) now
holds. However, the inability of the NPF to account for payments
by contributors over the past five years is a cause for serious concern – as to whether this type of change can be implemented.[11]
Investment in indexed mortgages would be a significant improvement for its savers.

Once again, Ghana has confronted a similar policy situation. Ghana
implemented a three-year pilot housing-finance project to establish
the Home Finance Company Ltd (HFC), which would implement a
mortgage system aimed at moderate and middle-income households.
The HFC is owned and operated on a commercial basis by The
National Bank of Ghana. To finance the mortgage system, the HFC
floats 30-year mortgage-backed housing bonds, which are subscribed
to by the government and the social security fund. The proceeds
from the bonds are lent to approved Originating and Servicing
Institutions (OSIs) for mortgage lending to households meeting specific
eligibility requirements.

Operating under a Dual Index Mortgage (DIM) system, repayments are based on 25 percent of verifiable household income through
a payroll deduction scheme, and the outstanding principal on all
bonds and mortgages is indexed to inflation on a monthly basis.
This system has already financed about 2000 modest (one to three
room) housing units. Private-sector developers design, market, and
build these houses on a commercial basis. It is hoped that the pro-

gram will ultimately help finance the sale of about 1000 existing government-owned housing units to the private sector as part of a long-term effort to restructure the huge, inefficient housing parastatals. Exactly how this kind of lending can be made affordable to households, yet simultaneously attractive to lenders, was described more fully in Chapter 6, but the Mexican case seems particularly apposite.

In Mexico, high nominal interest rates during the 1980s made standard fixed-payment mortgages with high initial payments unaffordable to most home owners. In 1984, the Central Bank implemented the new 'dual-rate' mortgage instrument, described in Chapter 6, which is designed to make mortgage lending more attractive in an inflationary environment. In 1986 the World Bank made the first of four housing loans to various financial agencies in Mexico. While Ghana, Hungary, Turkey, and Poland have only recently implemented indexed mortgage systems, Mexico has been experimenting with such systems for almost a decade. In Mexico, indexed mortgage schemes are now an accepted means to finance housing. The World Bank has most recently supported these operations with the 1992 loan to the Housing Fund for Commercial Banks (FOVI).

FOVI is a trust fund within the Central Bank which was created to channel federal funds from the Central Bank to commercial banks to finance low-cost housing for low-income beneficiaries. FOVI is financed through loans from the Central Bank, federal government transfers, and retained earnings. Commercial banks acquire FOVI funds through a funds auction, and then offer mortgage financing to the home buyer at a variable rate of interest equal to the average cost of funds. The interest rate on all FOVI loans is recalculated monthly to reflect changes in the average cost of funds. The loan amount is linked to the homebuyer's household income, and the initial monthly payment is established as a percentage of the average loan amount. Subsequent monthly payments are adjusted as the minimum wage increases. If adjusted monthly payments are not sufficient to cover the accrued interest, the difference is capitalized, and the loan term is extended. However, if the life of the loan extends more than 20 years, FOVI assumes the outstanding balance. As part of the World Bank project, FOVI is currently working on a new indexation scheme that will reduce the contingent liabilities resulting from the 20-year limit of the mortgage term. Over the

Table 10.1   Dual-indexed mortgage systems[12]

	Expected inflation rate (%)	Down-payment (%)	Real interest rate on loans (%)[13]	LTV (%)	Loan maturity (years)	Spread over cost of funds (%)
Poland	40	25	6	80	30	3
Mexico	12	10–20	6.8	80–90	12–15	5
					25 max	
Ghana	25	20–30	2.5–3.5	80	15–25	1

Source: SARs (Poland, Ghana); SAR and Country Department (Mexico).

next five years, FOVI is expected to finance 32 000 housing units annually, at a yearly investment cost of US$400 million. Table 10.1 summarizes the indexed mortgage systems under implementation in Poland, Mexico, and Ghana.

10.5   AN ALTERNATIVE HOUSING-FINANCE POLICY

Indexation as a Means to Address the Mortgage Affordability Problem

As discussed earlier, indexation has much to recommend it, particularly relative to credit subsidies as a means of reducing mortgage affordability concerns. From this perspective, the objective for re-designing mortgage contracts is to eliminate financial constraints that impede the affordability of housing for lower- and moderate-income households. In Nigeria during the mid-1980s, when inflation was 5 percent per annum, the effect of interest rates on mortgage contracts was trivial; but at current inflation rates (about 30 percent), interest rates are so high that mortgage financing is unaffordable in nominal terms. To repeat the mantra of Chapter 6, the objectives of adjusting mortgage repayment schemes under inflation are not to produce more housing. Rather, it is to provide a financing vehicle so that those who can afford to, and so desire, can purchase homes.

Whether, in practice, this makes sense depends upon the context. In Nigeria, there has been some experience with the issues involved. Merchant bankers in Lagos have already developed and issued a convertible bond scheme to finance real-estate development. Hence, most of the principles involved could be applied much more simply to innovations in the form of the mortgage instrument. However, while mortgage indexation has been tried with limited success in a number of countries as an alternative to lowering interest rates, its failings have been frequent. The large premium on the parallel foreign exchange market in Nigeria suggests that more than the usual cautions obtain.

10.6 CONCLUSION

The primary prerequisite condition necessary for the development of a well-functioning shelter sector in Nigeria is a credible macroeconomic environment. At the sectoral level a prerequisite is to end unfair competition between private and public firms. The private sector cannot compete with public-sector institutions receiving massive government subsidies. And, while this is a necessary condition for a more efficiently run shelter sector, it is not sufficient. Even if public-sector firms were eliminated, the development of a housing finance system based on significantly underpriced credit will only create pressures for favoritism in access to the funds based on non-economic criteria. Such a result is the opposite of what a well-functioning market would produce. Hence, equally important as the privatization of state housing producers is the need to privatize the housing finance system, and base the delivery of mortgage credit on commercial, and well-capitalized, rather than coercive means. If the latter steps were carried out, then these commercially-sound institutions could develop a sustainable means of providing affordable finance. Adaptations of the NHP are available, and have recently been introduced in other countries.

On the other hand, proposals made to expand the supply of finance and state-housing corporation activity in Nigeria will extend the public sector in ways that have not worked. Indeed, the most important of the proposals adopted in the NHP are inconsistent with both the broader approach taken in the Structural Adjustment Program (SAP), and the efforts to develop greater private-sector participation in the economy. Proposals such as directed credit and increased tax approaches were often followed in other countries during the lower inflation days of the late 1970s and early 1980s. Like these proposals followed elsewhere, the Nigerian proposals also date from the low inflation days before the SAP began in 1986.[13] Nigeria, in fact, is introducing and strengthening policies that other countries have eliminated or significantly restructured while undergoing structural adjustment programs. Hence, it is not clear that this is an appropriate environment in which to introduce financial innovations (such as indexed mortgages) to make mortgages more affordable, particularly if these instruments would be used to fund clearly inefficient suppliers. Therefore, before making the housing finance system more private-sector oriented, it would be prudent to make sure that the objective of such a policy is to exploit the enormous efficiency gains for the sector, rather than just increase the size of the transfers to the sector.

While the objectives of the NHP are laudable, the measures proposed to achieve these objectives will most likely cause serious problems when implemented. As currently structured, the National Housing Fund, the financial component of the NHP, is an unsustainable transfer that will create significant problems for an already troubled financial system. It will also impose significant costs on wage earners who will pay for this system with the expropriation of the return as well as with a portion of their retirement savings. Finally, it is almost certainly a regressive system that will encourage an increased politization of the shelter sector. Hence, rather than contributing to a much greater private-sector role in the housing sector, this policy is likely to have the opposite result: it will broaden the public role in the financial sector, increase the public claims on wage earners, and it will likely reinvigorate public-housing producers. Alternatives are available and should be considered.

11 The World Bank Experience with Housing Finance

In the last ten years the World Bank has lent over US$3 billion for housing finance projects. A review of the Bank's experience with these projects can offer some perspective and insights on when and how such projects can be effective contributors to broader economic policies and the financial deregulation process. A control point of the review is to indicate that while the Bank's experience is complicated and variable, one maxim, however, remains valid: correctly structured housing finance systems can be expected to significantly improve the mobilization of financial resources, and the effective targeting of subsidies. These improvements, in turn, can help develop the sector so that the social concerns generated by poor housing conditions can be obviated.

11.1 AN OVERVIEW OF THE WORLD BANK'S HOUSING-FINANCE PORTFOLIO

The Role of Housing

Housing, as has often been said, is not only an economic good, it is also a basic human need. The link between health and housing conditions, for example, is well established (although hard to quantify). Slums and squatter housing tend to be the most visible signs of poverty in developed and developing countries. Thus, housing plays a role in the social policies of virtually all governments. The reach of housing and housing finance policies, as has been stressed throughout the book, are often far beyond those measured in traditional budget documents.

For example, housing is the main user of urban land. This use has placed housing in the center of government interventions aimed

159

at managing urban growth and creating a 'healthy' and 'livable' urban environment. A plethora of laws, codes, and regulations define the rights to build, use, sell, and rent houses. This regulatory framework often determines how different actors on the housing market – builders, real-estate agents, owner-occupiers, renters, and landlords – respond to various social, fiscal, and financial sector policies.

In addition, because housing is so long-lived and costly relative to household income it is heavily dependent on household ability to borrow. Of all the social sectors, it is the capital-intensive housing sector that has been at the intersection of social policy and financial policy, often with adverse consequences for both sectors. The expansion of Bank lending for housing finance is largely a reflection of a desire to create a clearer relationship between not only social and financial sector issues, but also with urban development and fiscal concerns.

For Bank policy, these characteristics of the housing sector represent both a strategic opportunity, as well as a cause for serious concern. It is an opportunity because housing is, as argued in Chapter 2, one of the simplest – and safest – assets in the economy, and it is ubiquitously and increasingly demanded as economies expand. In this respect, market-rate housing finance can be an integral part of the Bank's effort to encourage private savings and support a process of financial-deepening in the economy. At the same time, if mortgage instruments are well designed, a functioning, competitive housing finance system can also reduce the need for government subsidies to all but the very lowest income groups.

On the other hand, such assistance is also a cause for basic concern because as the Bank *Housing Sector Policy Paper* (1975) stated:

> It is clear from the record that . . . [housing finance] assistance is fraught with many dangers . . . the failure to evaluate housing-finance institutions in the context of housing markets and the financial environment has led to heavy subsidies for housing for middle and upper-income groups . . . outdated financial policies frequently result in implicit subsidies . . . [that] are particularly unfortunate in housing . . . The Bank Group's contribution to housing finance therefore, has to be carefully formulated and executed if it is to avoid such pitfalls.

When financial institutions provide transfers rather than access to market-rate credit, they do not contribute to the development process. Indeed, they undermine it. Hence, a key aspect of the Bank's strategy in the sector is developing a well-defined understanding of how the sector and the institutions and regulations that govern it interact with the economy. Today, after more than 20 years of Bank experience and over 100 shelter projects in 60 countries, it is fair to say that Bank-supported squatter upgrading and sites-and-services projects have been a considerable improvement over the public-shelter programs that preceded them. These projects provide unquestionable evidence that production of affordable and adequate housing for the poor is possible. However, their achievements notwithstanding, it is clear that neither sites and services nor upgrading by themselves can provide a long-term answer to the problems of accommodating the growing numbers of urban dwellers. Much more fundamental change in policies, institutions, and incentives is necessary if resources are to be mobilized to meet the demographic demands for housing in developing countries.

Evolution of the Housing-Finance Portfolio

In the years since the Bank's first housing finance project, more than 30 projects focusing on housing finance or including major housing finance components have been approved, totaling over US$3.0 billion. Indeed, within 6 years of the first housing finance loan the volume of Bank lending for housing finance already exceeded the total 16-year volume of sites-and-services lending since the first such project in 1972.

In terms of regional variation in projects, Latin America (LAC) and Asia have the largest dollar share of housing-finance lending, but measured in terms of number of projects, the Africa region has a similar level of activity as LAC and Asia. The Europe and the Middle East (EMENA) region lags in both volume of housing-finance lending and number of projects. However, with recent projects in Poland, Albania, and Russia, this situation is changing.

Selection of Intermediaries

Over 80 percent of housing finance projects were channelled to financial intermediaries rather than to non-financial public-sector housing authorities. In addition, in the cases in which projects relied on government housing programs – Korea, Thailand, Chile, and Mexico – a central objective of the projects was a refocusing of the public-housing sector authorities so that the financial sector could more actively participate in the mortgage market. While this refocusing of the public sector took a number of different forms, the central objectives have been to reduce the overall level of subsidies and to better target them on lower-income families. In Mexico, Chile, Morocco, and Zimbabwe, follow-up housing finance projects carried this disengagement of the public sector from lending one step further.

Most of the institutions that received housing finance loans have either been created in recent years or considerably refocused. Cumulatively, these figures suggest that the borrowing institutions for shelter projects are now more likely to be financial intermediaries than public-housing entities, and they are likely to be newly created or recently restructured institutions.

11.2 AN ASSESSMENT OF THE EFFECTIVENESS OF HOUSING-FINANCE OPERATIONS

Any assessment of housing-finance interventions on the overall development strategy of the Bank will depend on the perspective taken. This section will focus on how well the lending operations of the Bank have responded to three different areas of policy concern identified in Chapter 1. In particular, it will attempt to answer how Bank projects help address the following questions:

- First, is there a clear strategy for the reform and development of the housing-finance sector that is consistent with broader financial sector objectives?
- Second, is the strategy consistent with the objective of restoring fiscal balance and controlling and targeting subsidies?

- Finally, does the strategy promote a well-functioning housing market and help low-income families get access to adequate housing?

In evaluating the financial sector implications of projects, emphasis is placed on the project's performance with respect to domestic resource mobilization efforts. The statistics presented are therefore similar to those presented in other Bank evaluations of financial intermediaries. Attention is given to the projects' effects on borrowers' interest-rate policies, on their efforts to mobilize domestic financial resources, and the response to loan arrears. In addition, the effect on the government's contingents liabilities is also examined.

For fiscal policy concerns, attention is given to the level, transparency, and targeting of subsidies and again, the government's contingent liabilities. Finally, for housing sector concerns, the focus is on institution building, the regulatory environment, and the unit costs of the houses financed by the program. These concerns are less quantifiable than are the financial or fiscal policy measures, but no less important.

Financial Sector Objectives

Resource mobilization

Almost 80 percent of the projects attempt to promote savings mobilization; more than 60 percent of the housing-finance institutions that have received Bank loans have been able to mobilize most of their resources domestically. This result is in sharp contrast to the less than 10 percent of Bank-supported development finance institutions that did so through the 1980s. The latter result is also in contrast to the results of the sample of agricultural credit loans for the same time period. The sample indicated that only 12 percent of the agricultural projects surveyed attempted to promote savings mobilization.

The inflation-adjusted interest rates paid for funds mobilized at the time of the project appraisal were overwhelmingly non-negative, 90 percent. These results are important for institutions financing assets that yield non-tradeable services. The long-term resource base of such lenders must be domestic financial assets. These assets can be mobilized only by inducing savers to place their savings in those institutions. Whether these funds are mobilized directly, or by other intermediaries and then on-lent to the housing finance lender depends upon the type of financial infrastructure that exists. But, regardless of the type of system, positive interest rates are essential to provide long-term financial integrity to the intermediation process.

Risk exposure and contingent liabilities

Another perspective on how projects affected government presence and risk-taking in mobilizing financial resources is whether the project changed the government's domestic risk exposure. Such risks are of particular concern in longer-term lending, such as housing finance, because the risk to the government is, of course, affected if it is a depositor in the housing-finance institution, or if it guarantees other depositors. Moreover, in practice, it also assumes contingent liabilities – or 'moral obligations' to make up losses – if it sets lending interest rates or regulations which undermine the viability of the housing finance institution.

Only a few of the projects increased the government's risk exposure with respect to domestic (as opposed to foreign exchange) contingent liabilities. In addition, of the projects that did increase the government's domestic contingent liabilities, other desirable objectives were usually achieved. This kind of loan, in effect, replaced a financing mechanism that ultimately conferred large credit subsidies with a mechanism that provides much smaller liabilities whose cost may but probably will not be realized.

Arrears

Before discussing the arrears-rate experienced by Bank-funded, housing-finance institutions, it is worth emphasizing that definitional and measurement issues in this area limit the strength of the conclusions than can be drawn. With this caveat in mind, a number of features nevertheless appear to be noteworthy:

• The average percent of portfolio arrears reported for housing finance institutions identified for Bank projects is on the order of 10 percent. This figure is better than the 16 percent rate realized by development finance institutions.

• Most of the projects appeared to have portfolios of commercial quality, that is, arrears of less than 6 percent of the portfolio.

In addition, (1) the average expected spread for all projects was about 3.0 percent, and according to simple measures of expected inflation, the real interest-rate charged was on the order of 3.6 percent; (2) the apparent commercial level borrowing-rate on so many of the projects stands in sharp contrast to the results reported in Malpezzi and Mayo (1987b) for Bank-financed shelter projects in the 1970s. Their analysis shows that the average on-lending rate for shelter projects was negative 3 percent for the 1972–81 period.

An obvious implication of moving to market-rate lending – as the housing finance projects appear to be doing – is concern for the target audience of beneficiaries. That is, as borrowing costs increase, the poor may no longer be able to afford to participate in housing programs. This result, in turn, raises the issue of how subsidy targeting or fiscal policy concerns are addressed in housing finance projects.

Fiscal Policy Concerns

Fiscal policy concerns were the primary objective of a quarter of the housing finance projects. These projects were concerned largely with the broader effects of housing subsidies on government expenditures and transfers. For example, the Malawi project was initiated by earlier structural adjustment discussions. Similarly, the Chilean project and the Mexican loans were components of broader fiscal policy dialogues between the Bank and the borrower.

While both of these projects were directed at the fiscal aspects of subsidy targeting, an equally important dimension was their reduction in the implicit taxes on the financial institutions which financed these subsidies. In Mexico, commercial banks were required to allocate an amount in the order of US$400–700 million per year to fixed-rate, low interest-rate mortgages. The Bank loan financed a time slice of commercial bank mortgage lending that eliminated much of this implicit tax on the banks. The elimination of this implicit tax was the product of a dialogue between the Bank and the government of Mexico. High quality studies of this issue were produced by the Mexicans and provided a key input into policy discussion.

Subsidizing target beneficiaries

A number of the fiscal features of the projects were prominent:

1. The target beneficiaries of housing-finance projects are 'below-the-median incomes' households, rather than the very poor. More than half of the projects provide cross subsidies to lower-income borrowers. One assumption seems to be that if lower- and middle-income households can be accommodated by debt at commercial rates, subsidies that had been going to them could then be redirected to those who truly need them. Finally, and perhaps most important, because of the relatively recent nature of the Bank's housing-finance projects, these projects could avoid the earlier errors of other sectors, and in principle at least build on lessons learned within 'other sectors'. For example, the Bank's experience in the agriculture sector has shown the ineffectiveness of attempting to help the poor through credit subsidies. In addition, the lesson learned from the Bank's sites-and-service projects is that the production of low-cost affordable housing is possible. If the right housing standards are in place, it is access to credit, rather than concessional lending terms, that can best improve housing conditions; and
2. A number of institutions that have been supported by housing finance projects provide access to concessional finance for very expensive housing, even if the projects themselves do not. In some countries, projects financed mortgages of up to US$17 000. However, the institutions which receive Bank loans could finance mortgages of up to US$50 000 at preferential interest rates. There is no obvious rationale for these institutions to provide credit at preferential interest rates, even if the interest rates are set by a regional monetary board that sets financial policies across a number of countries. It is exactly this concern that the Bank's *Housing Sector Policy Paper* (1975) warned against.

Besides the subsidy targeting concerns associated with housing-finance projects, an equally important concern is the efficiency with which housing transfers are mobilized. For example, forcing financial institutions to invest in the below-market interest-rate securities which ultimately finance housing loans – as has been done in many countries – is a reliance on a very inefficient transfer mechanism. Such devices can in the long run seriously erode the ability of financial systems to mobilize resources. Greater subsidy transparency not only yields a better measure of who is the subsidy beneficiary, it also yields a better sense of how government policy is affecting financial development. It helps give a sense of whether the borrower's subsidy is borne by the government, other borrowers (through higher interest rates), or deposits (through negative interest rates).

Foreign exchange risk

In only one case was the foreign exchange risk imposed on the borrowing intermediary. In almost 60 percent of the projects the government took the foreign exchange risk. The risk-bearing arrangements appear to impose more uncompensated risk-bearing on the government than do the arrangements made for industrial finance loans through financial intermediaries. In the latter type of project the government took the foreign exchange risk without fee in only half of the cases whereas they did so in 60 percent of the housing finance loans. On the other hand, the figure for housing-finance projects is similar to the figure for the sample of agricultural credit loans, that is, 64 percent of the projects.

Housing investments produce either no pecuniary income or rental income denominated in local currency. In addition, mortgage payments can make up as much as 25–30 percent of household income that is earned in local currency. Consequently, in the case of housing it is not possible for the ultimate borrower to carry the foreign exchange risk. Over the longer term such projects should clearly encourage domestic resource mobilization to finance housing. In this regard, the projects in Zimbabwe and Lesotho, which aimed for 100 percent domestically-based resource mobilization had noteworthy aspirations: all housing finance was to be domestically mobilized. In the short run, because housing-finance institutions finance domestic assets they are not able to effectively and directly bear foreign exchange risk. Thus, normally, the government should be willing to assume this risk for a fee. However, if the housing-finance institutions – and, by implication, the final borrower – do not pay a fee for the transfer of this risk, or pay a fee that is lower than the expected cost of this risk, the subsidy element should be recognized.

Housing Sector Concerns

The most frequent rationale for housing finance projects is sectoral
policy concerns. These concerns arise because of the inability of
most housing production delivery-mechanisms to accommodate the
large and growing demand for housing. For example, in many countries, and particularly in sub-Saharan Africa, the informal sector plays
the dominant role, not only in the provision of housing service, but
also in providing the inputs into housing production, the financing
that is used to purchase the housing, and even the titling of the
property itself. Obviously, in such environments housing sector concerns cut across Bank concerns with financial policy, employment
policy, fiscal policy, local administrative policy as well as, ultimately,
sectoral policy. Consequently, the characterization of rationales in
Table 11.1 understates the importance of sectoral concerns in gen-
erating such projects. In almost every instance in which financial or
fiscal policy concerns were the basic policy objective, these broader
concerns were generated by side effects of the functioning of the
housing and housing-finance delivery-mechanisms. Only in the cases
of Malawi and Albania were the projects developed without prior
housing-sector work or extensive technical assistance studies.

Those projects in which sectoral, policy-oriented objectives were
identified as the foremost rationale for the project can be subdivided into two sub-objectives:

1. Efforts to demonstrate that many lower- and moderate-income
   households can afford to repay market-rate finance. These efforts,
   in many respects, involve giving greater attention to the design
   and implementation of both effective mortgage and building
   practices.
2. Efforts to give greater emphasis to the private sector in providing
   both housing and housing-finance services. These efforts often
   seek to disengage the public sector from functions that the private sector can perform.

Evaluating the sectoral performance of housing-finance projects
against these kinds of objectives is more difficult than is the evaluation of their financial or fiscal performance for two reasons: first,
because the constraints on the development of more effective hous-

Table 11.1   Chief rationale for housing-finance projects

Financial sector-reforms	Broader fiscal policy initiatives	Housing sector concerns	
Côte d'Ivoire	Chile	Albania	Nigeria
Ecuador	Chile II	Argentina	Papua New Guinea
India	Ghana	Fiji	Philippines
Mexico II	Malawi	Indonesia	Russia
Morocco	Mexico	Korea	Thailand
Sénégal	Mexico I	Lesotho	Vanuatu
	Poland	Mexico	Zimbabwe
		Morocco	

ing-finance systems vary so widely depending on characteristics of the economy; and second, because these kinds of constraints are difficult to quantify in simple, summary statistics. Nevertheless, even though these kinds of characteristics may be difficult to measure they are important, if not fundamental, to the development of successful housing-finance projects.

11.3   IMPLEMENTING POLICY CHANGE

Linkages with Broader Financial Sector Strategies

The evolution of the housing-finance projects in Morocco provides a good example of how the implementation of Bank housing-finance projects is changing, both as the Bank's financial policy perspective changes and as problems of implementation affect project design. The 1983 housing-finance project in Morocco was very much in the image of the traditional development bank operation that preceded the 'Financial Intermediation Policy Paper'. It closely fol lowed the directed-credit paradigm that had been applied in virtually all Bank lending to financial institutions up to that time. Little emphasis was given to the specialized, housing bank's (Credit Immobilier et Hotelier, CIH) ability to mobilize resources directly from households. Instead, CIH remained as a residual borrower, financed by the earmarked investments of other financial intermediaries. The implementation experience (the project disbursed slowly) also clearly demonstrated that a number of land-management-related bottlenecks were major factors limiting the access of the poor to adequate housing. Lack of clear titles, cumbersome zoning and building regulations, and lagging infrastructure provisions, all interacted to reduce the supply of low-income housing.

The focus of the 1995 work on housing finance in Morocco moves beyond the directed credit paradigm. Although the current perspective does not address directly questions on the speed of financial liberalization, it is designed to 'fit' the housing-finance system into what will eventually be a market-determined financial system. It focuses explicitly on competitiveness and the ability to mobilize resources so that housing finance can ultimately operate without any government assistance in a fully liberalized financial system. In particular, the change in perspective has permitted the Bank to engage in a discussion of what types of financial instruments can best serve these purposes at the same time that other Bank interventions are aimed at resolving the land-management-related bottlenecks.

This kind of broader discussion of financial policy issues was not possible under the Bank approaches that supported the *status quo* of uncompetitive, highly-regulated financial systems. However, while it is now possible to engage in such discussions, it is important to stress that housing-finance reforms are only one part of a changing, financial policy environment. Equally important is that these reforms are only one component of housing-sector policy. As such, housing-finance reforms need to be evaluated in the context of an evolving financial system and sectoral policy. The evolution of housing policy in Mexico is another example of a sustained dialogue between the Bank and the borrowing country in which both parties cooperated in a joint effort to build a sustainable system of financial resource mobilization for housing.

As the data indicate, housing-finance loans can be made at positive real-rates through reliance on domestic resources, and with reasonable expectation for satisfactory cost recovery. However, it should be recognized that the development of more competitive. sound financial practices are long-term objectives. They may not be achievable in one project, particularly when housing-sector and financial-sector policies either are at odds with each other or have been carried on through fragmented policies for a number of years. In many countries, lasting improvements in the functioning of these sectors will require an incremental approach as has been pursued in Morocco. Similarly, follow-up housing-finance projects have been prepared in Zimbabwe, Chile, and Mexico, and more are planned for reforming socialist economies such as Russia, China, and Albania.

Another example of a housing-finance project that fosters the Bank's financial intermediation strategy is the loan to Ghana. This project, as described in Chapter 10, provides for a new mortgage instrument that permits household debt to replace large implicit credit subsidies in a heavily indebted country. It provides for the indexation of mortgage repayments to wages, and recognizes that in an economy such as Ghana's, real wage decreases may well imply temporary repayment problems for borrowers, but they do not necessarily imply a reduced long-term ability to repay. As a result, under the project, if real wages behave in such a way that repayments are not sufficient to amortize the loan, the shortfall can be capitalized into the outstanding loan balance. Simulations of various future, real-wage scenarios indicate that as long as inflation does not get out of hand, even with very pessimistic assumptions the indexation scheme can eliminate subsidies.

If this instrument becomes more broadly operative than it already is, it is likely to be a good example of a financial innovation that helps both the sector and the financial system. It shows how the development of mortgage instruments that are in tune with macroeconomic conditions can help ensure that lending institutions have competitive access to resources. These resources can be mobilized in reaction to demand and can help keep the need for subsidies to a minimum.

11.4   HOUSING-FINANCE PROJECTS AND SUBSIDIES

As has been stressed throughout, credit policies and regulatory controls generate large and unmeasured transfers to the sector, and as the scale of these transfers increases, this aspect of housing-finance policy has received greater emphasis. As 'The Bank's Approach to Subsidies' paper has argued and the housing-finance projects in Mexico and Chile have shown, transfers to the sector should and can be reduced by better-targeted, more transparent transfers. Over the near term, measurement and control of these subsidies will be important components of both the Bank's policy dialogue in this area and the Bank's research efforts.

Developing housing-finance institutions that minimize these subsidies will be central to this agenda. An important element will be the demonstration of how the newer analytical tools that are emerging to deal with these credit subsidies in developed countries can be applied to developing countries. For example, evidence of the Bank's ability to assess sector performance is provided by a comparison of the Bank's first housing-finance study in the Philippines (1982), with the most recent shelter study of Russia (1995). The latter study attempts to identify the factors that hinder the effective and more spontaneous development of the housing market. It attempts to deal with the basic questions posed in the Bank's subsidy paper that need to be addressed in any evaluation of government transfers. It shows that in Russia many of these impediments are in the regulation of the housing and land markets; others are in the housing-finance system. In this respect, it suggests that while Russian housing-finance policies are a source of implicit subsidies to upper-income borrowers, they are nevertheless of less importance than property rights issues: only by expanding the supply of housing and land with secure tradable titles can families gain access to adequate housing at affordable prices. Simultaneously, it also recognizes that in the move to expand finance for housing, the poor can not be forgotten.

The Philippines study, on the other hand, did not give explicit recognition to the economic costs of providing subsidies to the sector. The report never mentioned that the government's interest-rate policies were indicated by 'social' considerations and were often negative in real terms. The conclusions of the project completion reports for the two first shelter projects in the Philippines (issued in 1986 and 1987), however, accurately summed up the situation: '... negative financial returns represent a serious constraint to the replicability of the projects ... and the high-level of inflation has decapitalized the institutions'. Not surprisingly, it went on to say that 'there has been ... lack of an effective dialogue between the Borrower and the Bank on several important sector issues such as housing-finance ...' during the late 1970s and early 1980s.

Housing-Finance Projects and Housing-Sector Objectives

The Bank is still in a transition from a traditional housing-sector analysis, which looked at the demand side in terms of 'housing needs' and which emphasized the role of government as 'the' provider of shelter services, especially for the poor, to a broader analysis that puts housing and the government's housing policies in a broader economic perspective. This shift in perception has been followed by a shift in lending approach. However, the transition away from sites-and-services and upgrading projects to include housing-finance operations will not occur rapidly; nor, in many countries, should it occur at all in the near term. Most of the Bank's early shelter loans were made to lower-income African countries that were urbanizing rapidly, had very basic financial systems, and often had severe land rights problems. The average *per capita* income-level of countries receiving a sites-and-services project was 40 percent less than that of the countries receiving housing-finance loans. In most of the lowest-income countries, the sites-and-services approach was the appropriate strategy then, and in many of these countries it remains the appropriate strategy today.

Almost every housing-finance project was preceded by other kinds of shelter projects to build up the basic institutional infrastructure, and in most of the borrowing countries new or refocused institutions are the borrowing agency. In many respects, then, housing-finance projects represent a 'second generation' approach that should not be of the foremost priority for many of the Bank's lowest-income borrowers. However, just as the major rationale for the Bank's early sites-and-services projects was to demonstrate that the building standards of developed economies were inappropriate for developing nations, a broader rationale exists for the housing-finance agenda in these countries. In countries with little sectoral or financial infrastructure, it is important to demonstrate:

- the inappropriateness of specialized, continually and implicitly subsidized mortgage lenders; and
- the ability of moderate-income households to repay market loans.

In summary, it appears that some regional specialization of basic housing-finance strategies will almost inevitable occur. The same type of housing project that is appropriate or even essential in one type of country will be inappropriate, or of much lower priority, in another. For example, in many higher-inflation countries better mortgage indexation may be essential to make housing affordable, to reduce transfers, and to help mobilize financial resources. In such an economy, housing-finance interventions should be of relatively high priority. On the other hand, if a high inflation country also has a low level of economic and financial development, declining real income and a weak land-cadastral system, there are almost certainly many more important sectoral policy issues to be addressed before indexation is introduced or discussed. Stopping the leakage of resources through negative *ex ante* interest rates is essential in all high inflation countries. But whether mortgage indexation is the appropriate means of doing this is another question.

12 Conclusion

There are perhaps two central messages in the preceding chapters. First, housing-finance delivery mechanisms are often complex institutional structures that depend in large part on the accumulation of the accidents of history. Nigeria's system, for example, is quite different from that of Poland or Argentina. It follows that evaluation of these institutions is very country-specific and idiosyncratic, akin perhaps to a form of financial anthropology. Unfortunately, such a field of study does not lend itself to easy generalizations.

Fortunately, the second message is more encouraging. It is that despite the significant differences, there are often strong, underlying similarities across groups of countries. Furthermore, almost universally these systems are in a state of considerable flux. From this message some common, evaluative principles can be developed which can be applied in most circumstances.

To try to give a sense of these principles this chapter presents guidelines on housing finance presented by a recent World Bank policy work on *Housing: Enabling Markets to Work* (1993). These guidelines provide a telescopic summary of the components of an effective housing-finance system. Indeed, they can be enumerated into a table of 'dos and dont's'. Obviously, this kind of distillation of principles cannot be rigorous or rigid, and it is meant more as a leitmotif of a sustainable system than as a prescription or set of rules. Consequently, before presenting this table, a brief detour is taken on how sector perspectives have changed, and the way these changes have been affected by the changes in the world environment discussed in the first chapter.

Housing-Finance and Financial-Sector Perspectives

World Bank lending for housing operates in a world environment that has changed in basic ways over the almost 25 years since such operations began. No longer is the Bank lending only to the lowest-income countries undergoing rapid urbanization. With the coming

of the debt crisis in 1982 came a fundamental change in the importance of improving domestic-resource mobilization capabilities. As
a result, the projects financed have become very different. The types
of borrowers have changed from exclusively public-sector institutions to financial intermediaries, and the loans changed from being
small demonstration projects to large loans. Instead of focusing
exclusively on the physical characteristics of the assets financed that
characterized early lending, attention has now shifted to the institutional structure of the implementing agencies, and their ability to
mobilize and manage resources.

Not only did the Bank's counterparts change, so too did the Bank's
perspectives. The first Bank review of financial-sector policies was
undertaken in the late 1970s. This review was followed by the Bank's
early support for efforts at financial liberalization. Following these
efforts, similar attention was given to less centralized control in the
housing sector. Renaud (1984) stressed the importance of improved
resource-mobilization and institutional governance for providing shelter
on a sustainable basis. Tangible expression of these views began in
a range of housing-finance projects, beginning in 1982.

Since the early 1980s all Bank-supported urban projects, not just
the shelter projects, have moved towards greater reliance on finance.
Most urban projects now attempt to use either housing or municipal
finance to replace coercive efforts by governments to regulate and
directly fund household and local government investments. Inducement
rather than directive became the vehicle of support. In the urban
sector a clear shift in the type of lending has taken place, and in
lending for shelter, this shift has perhaps been the most pronounced.

This new approach, like the new approach to financial-sector lending,
gives considerable attention to the importance that policy distortions and local ownership can place on moving to more market-
oriented systems. It is perhaps no coincidence that this change in
approach followed immediately on the heels of the fall of communism
and the rise of democratically-elected and decentralized governments
throughout the world. The urban public institutions involved in Bank
projects are now more likely to be accountable institutions developed by democratically-elected constituencies. Similarly, the non
governmental organizations involved in implementing Bank loans
are more likely to be private-sector firms, as was the case in shelter
projects in Ghana and India. Both the public and private institu-

tions involved are much more demand-responsive than were counterparts during the early years of Bank urban lending.

These new Bank counterparts are also considerably more likely to be operating in a financial system that is more competitive and open to intersectoral resource flows. But, also like development finance institutions, the institutions involved in shelter finance are still sometimes financially weak. In the public sector they often continue to carry out ambiguously-defined and overlapping objectives, and typically act as agents of government rather than strictly as private intermediaries. Finally, as has been stressed throughout the preceding chapters, these institutions now operate in an environment that will compel them to be much more self-reliant.

Guidelines for Effective Housing Finance

With this brief historical detour in hand, consider the following guidelines for effective housing finance. Table 12.1, from the Housing Policy Paper, provides a summary statement of the 'dos and don'ts' of financial policy as it applies to housing finance.

Of course, each phrase in the table covers a multiple of issues that may be very difficult to achieve in a particular country context. It is easier said than done, for example, to suggest that lending should be done at positive real interest rates when the entire financial system does not follow such practices. Similarly, how can foreclosure laws be enforced when they do not exist or it takes the court system 10 years to operate? Nor is any guidance given about which should come first – for example, prudential regulation or private-sector lending. Nevertheless, the basic building blocks of an effective system are analytically relatively straightforward – even if the process of getting to such a system is one that may require considerable strategy.

The table says that shelter finance should be competitively supplied at market interest rates by prudentially-sound institutions. The institutions should operate in well-designed and transparent regulatory systems that provide adequate legal recourse for both borrowers and lenders. Inter-institutional lending should be based only on clear accounting standards and practices. Projects financed by these systems should be demand-determined, and, to the greatest extent possible, seek full cost recovery. In cases where projects are unlikely

Table 12.1   An enabling strategy for housing finance

Housing Policy. Housing demand may suffer due to lack of efficient institutions for creating and preserving private property rights, no effective system for recording ownership, and no system for providing stable long-term sources of housing finance. Housing supply may be unresponsive to demand due to under-investment in trunk infrastructure or due to existence of monopolies, which control the availability of land, building materials or residential construction.

Government can enable the housing sector to function well by focusing on seven operational instruments; three to stimulate housing demand, e.g., (1) developing property rights, (2) developing mortgage finance, (3) rationalizing subsidies, three to facilitate the process of housing supply, e.g., (1) providing infrastructure for residential land development, (2) regulating land and housing development, (3) organizing the building industry, and finally one to create an overall institutional framework for managing the housing sector and ensuring adequate access to housing for the poor. *Housing Finance Policy.* With regards to mortgage finance some generic 'dos' and 'don't's' are clear:

Dos and don'ts in developing mortgage finance

Do	Don't
+ Allow Private Sector to Lend	− Allow Interest-Rate Subsidies
+ Lend at Positive Market Rates	− Discriminate Against Rental Housing
+ Enforce Foreclosure laws	− Neglect Resource Mobilization
+ Ensure Prudential Regulation	− Allow High Default Rates
+ Introduce Better Loan Instruments	

Source: 'Housing. Enabling Markets to Work', World Bank Policy Paper, April 1993.

to or do not achieve full financial cost recovery, a clear source of either subsidy-funding or contingent risk-bearing should be identified at the outset. Finally, subsidies and finance should be identified and separated.

The preceding chapters suggest that the process of moving towards market-based, competitive housing-finance systems is in full train. As the processes of greater financial integration and more market-based public policy come into play, the methods of financing shelter will undoubtedly continue to undergo substantial change. This process of change will take many forms and will rarely come quickly. Nevertheless, it is worth remembering that the fits and starts of this process, as reflected in the stresses on existing institutions, are usually a response to underlying market forces.

It is also worth noting that establishment of a market-based system ultimately holds out more than the prospect of being able to use resources much more effectively. In some respects, the change in housing-finance systems around the world is much like the replacement of an old car with a newer model. But, in some important respects, this analogy breaks down. The old car simply won't work in the new environment. It is not a matter of *if* it will crash, but rather a matter of *when*. For safe driving in the new, high-speed environment, a car with a *better* design, not just a *new* car is needed. Consequently, housing-finance reforms should be pursued not only because they can provide efficiency gains and trickle-down distributional benefits. They should be pursued because they can help avoid serious economy-wide disruptions.

Notes

1 Introduction

1. Sylla (1991) provides details on the 1980s in an historical context.
2. See Mark Boleat (1985) for a discussion of housing finance institutions in a number of countries.
3. See Fabozzi and Modigliani (1992).
4. The savings and loan story in the US is well known. More than 4300 federally insured institutions failed between 1980 and 1991. Barth and Brumbaugh (1994). Similar, if less extreme pressures on existing institutions arose in a number of European countries. See Diamond and Lea (1992).
5. Tait and Heller (1982) for budget measures. See any Special Analysis of the Budget since 1986 for a discussion of US efforts to measure credit subsidies and obligations.

2 The Framework for Analysis

1. Goldsmith (1985) offers the most complete discussion of this kind of data. Ibbotson and Siegel (1983) estimate that real-estate accounts for approximately one-third of the world market wealth portfolio.
2. Goldsmith (1969). In 11 of the countries examined by Goldsmith, it is possible to identify (approximately) the share of mortgages in financial assets. The countries and their average share of financial assets in mortgages in the early twentieth century was 21 percent with a median share of 11 percent.
3. US Department of Commerce (1987) estimates the service life of residential investments in one- to four-unit structures to be 80 years, the longest-lived asset. In contrast, industrial buildings have a service life of 31 years.
4. Cunningham and Hendershott (1984) focus on the optimal mortgage default strategy. The authors suggest that in the United States the indirect transactions costs of defaulting should be on the order of 20 percent of the loan amount.
5. Fons (1987) shows that US investors received a yield differential of 3.5 percent for holding corporate debt that was not of AAA quality relative to the AAA-rated debt. This implies a credit risk fee seven times the 0.5 percent charged to mortgagors.
6. The World Bank (1985) indicates that one-third of the development finance institutions that received World Bank loans were technically insolvent.

180

7. See the 1988 regulatory requirements recommended by the Bank for International Settlements. They identify mortgages as being much less risky financial assets. Ironically, one of the most significant mispricing of risks that occurred in the world financial system in recent years was that of the savings and loan associations. However, the mispricing was due to the structure of deposit insurance and not the type of lending undertaken.

8. Goldsmith (1985). The countries are the United Kingdom, United States, Germany, and France.

3 The Fiscal Policy Dimension

1. Tait and Heller (1982) empirically analyze eleven categories of government expenditures in 92 countries. They present 'predicted' and realized values of government expenditures for each of the different categories. The coefficient of variation for their models' predicted value of government expenditures on housing and community development relative to the realized value was the second largest of all the sectors.

2. The World Bank Policy Paper on Financial Intermediation (1985) shows that for a sample of 35 developing countries the average inflation rate over the 1974–84 period increased from 7 percent to 25 percent per year. From 1983–7, the average inflation rate doubled again to 50 percent. See World Development Report (1989).

3. Since McKinnon (1973), the $M2$ to GDP ratio has been used as one of 'the simplest measures of the importance of the monetary system in the economy' (p. 91).

4. See Morris (1985) or Chakarvarty (1985).

5. Between 1972 and 1985 the average deficit of developing economies increased by almost 50 percent to more than 4 percent of GDP. See table 23 of the World Development Report 1987.

6. Gottlieb (1976) shows that for many Western European economies and the US the production of housing has been one the more volatile components of GDP. Hence, control of credit to this credit intensive sector can be expected to minimize the volatility of GDP growth.

4 The Real Sector Dimension

1. Renaud (1991) shows that in the late 1980s the simple average gross rent-to-income ratio for Bulgaria, China, Hungary, Poland, Romania, the former Yugoslavia and the USSR was less than 3 percent. Similar figures hold for Czechoslovakia (Kingsley and Struyk, 1992). Administered rent levels are even lower when measured as a fraction of economic rent because income in the PCPEs was also severely repressed. In market economies, in contrast, the average rent-to-income ratio generally exceeds 20 percent (Mayo and Angel, 1992).

2. The Russian Republic has identified housing as one of its most foremost reform areas, and in 1991 adopted a law 'On Privatization of the REFSR Housing Stock' (Kalinina, 1992). One of Poland's first loans from the World Bank was a $200 million housing loan; in both 1988 and 1991 the Chinese embarked on major housing reform effort (World Bank, 1991a); and a number of World Bank studies of housing policy in Eastern European countries have pointed out the broader problems posed by socialist housing-delivery systems, and the need to reform these systems.

3. China's 1991 plans are based on a premise that it will take until the year 2015 to develop a housing market and that privatization will not occur on a significant scale for at least 10 years.

4. This is a general theme of McKinnon (1991): 'Indeed, the tendency of the fiscal position of the government to deteriorate because of the liberalization itself militates against any 'giveaways' of industrial assets or the housing stock' (p. 148).

5. See Renaud (1991) for a more complete description of these subsidies and their relative use, for example, among public housing, cooperatives and private dwellings, and Tanzi (1991) for the taxes.

6. Renaud (1991) finds households' mobility in reforming economies to be less than 10 percent of market economies. Again, see Blanchard *et al.* (1991) for a discussion of the potential costs of this impediment to restructuring.

7. McKinnon (1991, pp. 37 and 52) suggests that the hurdle rate for new investments in the converting economies should be near this value.

8. As first step, dividends equal to $fin/(1 - \tau)$ on a stock valued at reproduction cost could be allocated to subsidies. If households used part of their subsidies to consume non-housing goods or if PCPEs have overinvested in housing, market-clearing rent levels will be below long-run equilibrium levels. Subsidies would then have to be cut temporarily to reflect the below-market return on existing housing capital. Over time, an excess of absorption over net new construction would increase rents toward the long-run equilibrium level, and subsidies would increase.

9. The state need not give away all publicly owned units. The share of public housing in the total housing stock in market economies varies from 2 percent in the US to 30 percent in Britain (Renaud, 1991, p. 38, note 15). The criteria for robust private markets is that public housing not be an alternative at a subsidized rate.

5 A Simple Theory of the Policy Dimensions of the Housing Sector

1. The net level of public housing production can be used as an approximation of the level of additions to the stocks of alternative tenures particularly in cases where policies discourage production of private rental units.

2. Equation (5.2) could also be adjusted by θt as was equation (5.1). However, such an adjustment does not change any of the results, and just adds another term. Moreover, because of the cash-flow constraint imposed by nominal mortgage contract arrangements, one could, as has Kearl (1979), argue that the nominal cost of funds is the relevant price for potential mortgagors.

3. This approach is taken for simplicity; a simultaneous equation approach could also be used.

4. The model could be simplified, and perhaps made more realistic if we assumed that the mortgage market was supply constrained. In such a model $i_H = C - MS/e$ and only (5b) remains ambiguous. This simplification was not made so that some of the possible linkages between the housing and capital markets could be demonstrated. In addition, the i_H solved for in equation (5.3) could also be viewed as a below market rate of interest that is a function of the market rate.

5. The assumption that nominal rates increase by θ is consistent with findings for the US. In this case the return on home-ownership rises at a faster rate than the increase in the cost of capital. This assumption implies a'3 > 0. However, there is empirical support in the US for the opposite contention, i.e., a'3 < 0. In our stylized steady-state we are positing that as θ increases the return to home-ownership becomes increasingly more important relative to whatever institutional constraint cause a'3 < 0, so that the latter becomes weaker.

6. Mortgage demand is derived from the demand for housing and most houses have less than 100 percent finance. In addition, at higher income levels, particularly with the imposition of mortgage interest deduction limits, one would expect more of internally generated funds. The model could be easily modified to accommodate notions of permanent income and/or various lags in one or more markets. See Laidler (1968).

6 The Financial Dimension: Competition for Deposits

1. See, for example, Friedman (1974a, b) for such a claim. On the other hand, for a prescient article on the potential problems with the forms of indexation in use in Brazil, see Fishlow (1974).

2. See Cardoso and Dornbusch (1987) and Heyman (1987) on deindexation in Argentina and Brazil, respectively. See Veneroso (1983) for a discussion of the Chilean housing finance case and Silveira (1989) for a discussion of housing finance in Brazil. World Bank mission reports describe the situation in Paraguay. McNelis (1988) provides a broader discussion of indexation and deindexation for a number of countries.

3. Colombia is a notable exception. See Currie (1987) or Chapter 7 for a discussion of this case. The Mexican case was one in which until the late 1980s wage indexation was used for subsidized credit and fixed nominal interest rate loans were provided through the banking system.

4. The United Kingdom, Canada, and some former British colonies are exceptions to this description as was the US prior to 1934. However, some Latin American countries started to index loan repayments (Chile in 1959, Brazil in 1964, Colombia in 1972, Paraguay in 1973, and Argentina 1976), fixed payment loans were the common financing vehicle in most countries.

5. For a review of the repayment tilt problem and international experience with indexation see Lessard and Modigliani (1975).

6. Data on the inflation rate in developing countries from World Bank, World Development Report (1992), p. 63.

7. The Colombian system has worked very effectively for over 20 years during which time inflation was in the 20 to 30 percent annual range. See Chapter 7.

8. Buckley *et al.* (1989). The income levels needed to buy a house are those sufficient to amortize a loan with a given percent of income, that is 25 percent. Lenders could of course increase this ratio and thereby permit a means of adjusting to the cash-flow problem. In practice, however, this kind of adjustment is rarely made. One explanation for the lack of this kind of adjustment is that the increase in this ratio would increase the risk and hence the required interest rate at a faster rate.

9. This income figure corresponds to approximately the 60th to 70th percentile of urban households. The calculation of this household's location in the income distribution must be viewed as a very rough approximation. For reference, however, consider the following: Turkish *per capita* income in 1987 was US$1 150 and family size of five yielding an average household of US$5 800. If urban incomes are 20 percent higher than this national figure, average urban family income is approximately US$7 000 per year, US$1 000 more than the annual income of our representative beneficiary.

10. The wage data come from various World Bank Country Economic Memoranda.

11. The Argentina experience is detailed in Chapter 8; Brazil's housing-finance problems are detailed in Silveira (1989).

12. See Maydon *et al.* (1988) on the Mexican case and Chapter 10 for a discussion of the Ghana case.

13. An important feature of the loan term setting is that a payment factor is selected such that: (1) the loan would fully amortize in a period less than the extended maturity period if there are no real-wage reductions, and (2) the amount of term extension to cushion the possible, real-wage reductions is such that the extended loan fully amortizes after accounting for the anticipated possible, real-wage shocks. If these conditions are not fulfilled the loan can introduce moral hazard into the contract. That is, borrowers could be induced to take 'too big' a loan because the risk of repayment at the end is not theirs.

14. For example, Lessard and Modigliani (1975) discuss the simultaneous use of real and nominal interest rates. Alternatively, a specific rate of

graduation of payments can be set at the outset of the loan with the interest rate indexed to nominal interest rates.

15. While any simple measure of the limits to indexation's effectiveness is arbitrary our cut off of 50 percent per annum as an upper limit receives empirical support from Cardoso and Fishlow (1989). In a cross sectional study of 17 Latin American countries, they show that at rates of inflation of less than 51 percent *per annum* there is no systematic effect of inflation on growth – except in one period during which it is positive. They also show that if the sample is not limited to inflation rates below 50 percent, there is a negative correlation between inflation and growth.

16. For example, if the contract is viewed as a mortgage with a put at maturity, the put would be priced by a well-functioning market. Alternatively, even if the state accepts this contingent transfer, it is clearly a more efficient way to subsidize mortgage credit, if that is thought to be desirable, than is an interest-rate reduction.

7 The Financial Policy Dimension: Competition for Deposits

1. Data on M2\GDP for Argentina, Brazil, Chile, Colombia, Mexico, and Peru for the 1974–84 period indicate that all of these countries except Colombia, at least once experienced a substantial reduction in broadly-defined monetary balances as a share of GDP. The Colombian ratio was much less volatile, as well as almost monotonically increasing. In one year, 1979, there was a less than 1 percent decrease in $M2/GDP$. A log linear regression of $M2/GDP = Ae^{Ut}$, where t = time, for each of the six countries for the 1974–84 period (Mexico, only 1977–84) indicates that in Colombia the coefficient on time was positive and significant at the 1 percent level, and the $R2$ was equal to .68. The results for the other countries did not yield a significant time trend except for Brazil, but in Brazilian case, the coefficient was negative. Source for the data is International Financial Statistics.

2. The rate of return over the 1958–71 period is inferred from Carrizosa *et al.* (1982); the data for the later period are from Correa (1986). Berry and Urrutia (1976) also provide data on real-deposit rates and a discussion of the broader effects of mortgage lending policies in the pre-indexation period.

3. See Berry and Soligo (1980) for a discussion of the development strategy and Sandilands (1980) for a discussion of the CAVs creation and their early regulation.

4. Currie was formerly the chief advisor to both Mariner Eccles, Chairman of the Federal Reserve Board, and President Roosevelt. He also directed the first World Bank mission to Colombia in 1949.

5. The informal sector generally has three important dimensions: finance, employment, and housing production. In contrast to many other Latin

American economies, each of these aspects of the informal sector appeared to contract during the 1970s. See the World Bank (1987, p. 70) for further discussion of the expansion of the formal financial sector in the 1970s. With respect to housing, Urrutia (1985, p. 64) documents the very significant formalization of the housing stock that took place over the 1970s. The World Bank (1983a, pp. 19–23) provides a discussion of labor participation over the 1960s and 1970s saying that in the latter period the employment expansion would appear to be the highest achieved by a big country over a comparable period. After 1972 employment in the informal sector continued to grow more rapidly than did employment in the formal sector. However, it grew at a less rapid rate than in the 1958–72 period even though total employment expanded much more rapidly in the second period. Over the period 1958–72 the share of the labor force in the informal sector showed an increasing trend, expanding in all the years except in three, when the decrease was negligible. In the 1972–86 period, in contrast, the informal market share contracted in half the years even though the indirect costs of formal-sector employment increased sharply.

6. See Isaza (1987) for a complete listing of all the regulations governing CAVs since their creation, and Carrizosa *et al.* (1982) for a discussion of broader, financial-market policies that have affected the functioning of the CAVs.

7. Strictly speaking, the indexed time and savings deposits (CAVs) should be part of $M2$, but in our analysis, we separated the CAV deposits from $M2$ to isolate the effects of these deposits. The treatment, as far as taxes are concerned, of these two 'monies' $(M2-M1)$ and $(M3-M2)$ are identical from 1973 onwards.

8. The estimates are stylized for a number of reasons. Most importantly they use *ex post* measures of inflation rather than the *ex ante* rates that motivate the holdings of various types of balances. In addition, the assumption that real returns become completely invariant with respect to the inflation rate after indexation was introduced is an exaggeration. Complete insulation of real returns was not achieved, so that assumption lowers the estimated tax rate. On the other hand, however, we make no attempt to account for the blurring of distinctions between types of monies. This assumption causes the estimates of tax in the post-1972 period or err in the other direction. Finally, we assume that the real rate of interest was constant and equal to 2.5 percent throughout the period

9. These numbers were obtained by calculating average inflation rates and average inflation tax over the two time periods: 1958–72 and 1973–84. For the time period 1958–72 as described in the text, $T1$ was the inflation tax used and for 1973–84 period, $T2$ was the inflation tax used. The average inflation tax was divided by the average inflation rate to get these numbers.

10. Indeed, recent work by Dailami (1989) suggests that Colombian cor-

porations are making use of below-market, interest-rate credit to buy market-rate financial assets. His work shows that in 1983 financial assets accounted for 20 percent of total assets of non-financial corporations in Colombia. This figure is double the rate observed in developed economies.

11. See World Bank (1987) and (1983a) for discussions of the financial stress in Colombia. In 1982 this stress led to a financial crisis and the creation of a Fund to Guarantee Financial Institutions.

12. Romer (1987) raises doubts as to whether problems of simultaneity can be overcome by instrumental variables. He says 'there is little hope that valid instruments exist'. (p. 186)

13. We also estimated equations which adjusted the labor input for the effects that female participation rates and education would have in a manner suggested by Hanson *et al.* (1985). Similarly, we also constructed measures of the utilized capital stock relying on Cuddington's (1986) measures of permanent and cyclical measures of real GDP. We assumed that the capital stock was completely utilized in 1974, the year in which Cuddington estimates GDP was at the highest cyclical peak of our estimation period. In other years capital was assumed to be less than fully utilized by the same percent that cyclical output was less than output in the peak year. Equations estimated with these adjustments reduced the standard error of the equations and the regression coefficients. These results are not reported because of concern with *ad hoc* data transformations in an already highly aggregated equation.

14. To give a concrete example of our adjustment for equivalent units of monetary balances, suppose that in real terms 100 units of M are observed in both periods 1 and 2, and that the inflation rate was 5 percent higher in period 2. In this case the holder of monetary balances in period 2 would have to allocate more of his income to such balances to derive the same level of services. Just as the Darby effect indicates that nominal interest rates must increase by $1/1-T$ to keep real returns constant with respect to a change in the rate of inflation, our approach implies that equivalent units of monetary balances are similarly constant if they are adjusted by $1/1-T$ where $T = \theta$.

15. Like Khan and Ahmad (1985), we also estimated equations including a time trend as a representation of neutral, technological progress. Our results were similar to theirs. The coefficients of the other variables in the equation were not significantly different from zero. They suggest that this result seems to be caused by high collinearity. We also used a non-linear test for the appropriateness of the Cobb – Douglas specification as opposed to a CES functional form. Our results also provided strong support for the Cobb – Douglas specification.

16. The growth in output per unit of labor is decomposed into growth in capital per unit of labor, growth in monetary balances per unit of labor and the remainder is attributed to 'technical change'. When monetary balances are not included, growth due to capital per labor is 28 per-

cent and technical change, 72 percent. However, when monetary balances are included, growth due to capital is 21.5 percent, technical change, 35 percent and monetary balances, 43.5 percent. For more detail, see Solow (1957).

17. See Reyes (1987) for the most recent data on income distribution. Urrutia (1985) provides the most comprehensive evidence for the 1970s.

18. The Chenery and Syrquin (1975) work is a regression model of the behavior of 101 countries over the 1950–70 period. It 'explains' various characteristics of an economy, for example, employment in different sectors, urbanization, saving, and income distribution measures as a function of the level of *per capita* income and population. The basic perspective of the work is that development processes are sufficiently uniform among countries to produce a consistent pattern of change. The analysis provides measures for the behavior of a representative developing country. For Colombia, the model's predictions for employment distribution among primary, manufacturing and service sectors were very close to the observed values; so too were its estimate of savings and investment rates and the distribution of income.

19. It predicts that the share of income going to the lowest two quintals would decline slightly from 11.4 to 11.2 percent of income. By 1985, in the seven largest cities the households in the lowest two quintals received 12.8 percent. See Reyes (1987).

8 The Fiscal Policy Dimension: Implicit Subsidies

1. The features of the Argentine system which are common to other countries are: (1) the use of a tax fund to provide subsidized credit for housing; (2) the reliance on one of the largest depository institutions in the country to provide mortgage loans that are not completely indexed for inflation; and (3) real borrowing rates within the formal financial sector in excess of 10 percent per year. In addition to Argentina, such systems have been in operation in Brazil, Colombia, Mexico, Peru, and Turkey.

2. For housing data, and a longer-term perspective on the Argentine housing market see Yujnovsky (1984). The National Housing Plan of 1985 and Diaz-Alejandro (1970).

3. Khan and Ul Hague (1987) show that Argentina had one of the highest levels of capital flight. The data on Argentina are from various published World Bank reports, the World Development Report, and the Central Bank of Argentina. Computations on inflation from International Financial Statistics, December 1986 (Washington, DC: International Monetary Fund).

4. Source: For housing investment data, Argentine Housing Secretariat. The real borrowing-rate figure is from Boschen and Newman (1986).

5. Household formation exceeded production by more than 40 000 units

in 1985, after having exceeded production levels by an average of 15 000 units per year over the previous three years.

6. Figures on rents, house prices, and the number of units offered for rent are from Informe Mensual de Alquileres, (Monthly Report on Rents), Nacional de Investigacion y Desarrollo, July, 1986.

7. Data on FONAVI housing production and the income of beneficiaries are from Housing Ministry staff. The FONAVI housing cost estimate is from a UNDP Study. Australs were equal to 1.1 to the US$ in late 1986.

8. Source: Argentine Housing Ministry.

9. Source on the data for BHN is from the Central Bank of Argentina. The public deposits have accounted for 85 to 90 percent of the Bank's deposit base.

10. Source for house price trends in Greater Buenos Aires is a Housing Ministry survey. The coefficient of variation of the Argentine stock market index over the same period was 4.3 times larger than the coefficient of variation of house prices.

11. See Buckley and Gross (1985) for a review of this literature for the US, and Hendry (1981) for the UK.

12. See the Special Analysis of the Budget, Office of the President, Office of Management and Budget (Washington, DC) 1986, for a discussion of the recent attempts to measure the cost to government of various credit programs.

13. Such a result could occur if (1) net rents were equal to 8 percent of house value per year for 30 years, (2) housing's real net value were expected to be constant, and if the real interest rate were 4 percent and administrative costs for managing and collecting mortgage payments were 2.5 percent per year. With these assumptions, the rental payment stream would be discounted by 6.5 percent, and the store of value at 4 percent and the house would be worth 24 400 australs. The bases for the assumptions about net rent-to-value, land values, and real house prices are based on discussions in the Housing Ministry and surveys of rents and prices carried out by the Ministry. The imputed rent-to-value ratio is consistent with the empirical work of Malpezzi and Mayo (1987b) and similar to the assumptions made by Laidler (1969).

14. Specifically, I assume that the real rent increases observed in Greater Buenos Aires over 1980–5, and the roughly $3\frac{1}{2}$ per cent increase in real international, borrowing costs noted earlier, together caused households to expect to have to pay annual rents equal to 10 percent of the cost of the unit.

15. The assumption is conservative given that Diaz-Alejandro (1985) shows over the 1980–4 period the average real deposit-rate was negative and there are significant transactions costs to capital flight, particularly for small amounts of capital.

16. Source: On the total number of FONAVI loans, United Nations Development Programme analyses.

17. See Furstenberg (1976) for a discussion and estimation of the share of a counter cyclical US housing-finance subsidy that went to inframarginal households. His results indicate that over 85 percent of the subsidies were inframarginal and did not induce new production. They are consistent with Murray's (1983) empirical findings for the US. Because of the structure of the subsidy, a much smaller share of the Argentine subsidy recipients is likely to be marginal, new house buyers than was the case in the US program. Hence, the assumption of zero distribution of subsidies to marginal buyers, while obviously the lower bound of how many could have been affected, does not seem too unreasonable.
18. See Malpezzi and Mayo (1987a) for housing price and income elasticity estimates for developing countries. The calculations here assume that slightly fewer than 9 million Argentine housing units are worth 11 000 australs each. The figures on the share of wealth in housing and its relationship to GDP are consistent with similar figures for other countries presented by Goldsmith (1985).

9 The Fiscal Policy Dimension: Implicit Taxes

1. In a comprehensive analysis of the socialist system, Kornai (1992) makes a distinction between the stages of the classical and reform socialism. In the case of Hungary the classical socialist phase lasted from 1949 through 1963, reform socialist from 1963 through 1989; the post socialist transition started in 1989.
2. See Chapter 4 for a discussion of the components of this capital income and cost of services subsidy.
3. Hungary began implementing reforms to the classical socialistic system with the introduction of the New Economic Mechanism in 1968.
4. See World Bank (1991b).
5. For the US, see Hendershott and Hu (1980), Mills (1987), Poterba (1992), and White and White (1977); for the UK, see Minford *et al.* (1987) and Hills (1991); for Germany, see Mayo (1986) and Muellbauer (1992); and for Sweden see Brownstone and Englund (1988).
6. See Rosen (1979) or Poterba (1992).
7. See Hills (1991) for a discussion of the problems related to inferring subsidy levels from government expenditure data.
8. See Chapter 3 for an empirical review of housing investment *per capita* GDP across countries, and Chapter 4 for a discussion of over- or underinvestment in housing in socialist economies. See the World Bank (1991a) for the data on China.
9. These distributional issues can be very important, as White and White (1977) have shown for the US, but they are beyond the scope of this analysis. Here the focus is on how large the efficiency costs might be in the reforming economies.

10. See Hendershott and Hu (1980), Laidler (1969), and the review of UK studies by Hills (1991). Also see appendix to Chapter 9.

11. In addition, our measure of loss does not include the chronic shortage and arbitrary subsidies. The losses described cover only the part of the total welfare loss that would be traditionally measured in market economies. Another loss arises due to chronic excess demand, or what might be termed 'frustration loss'. To explain this consider Figure 9.1. Extend the demand curve downward up to the point where it intersects with the horizontal line belonging to the subsidized low rent H. Let us denote the point of intersection by K. The quantity demanded at this point is Q''. If supply were adjusted to demand at the existing rent H, then that would be the actually rented quantity. The would-be tenants are used to the rent level H. In the classical socialism of USSR the rent remained unchanged and absurdly low for decades. As a result, the would-be tenants – who are now in the eight-year-long waiting list for housing in Moscow do not get the missing quantity $Q/Q//$ – are frustrated and angry. They have also created a political constituency for the production of new housing to be rented out at traditional rent levels. The result is that in Russia, for example, a significant portion of new housing production is produced to attempt to satisfy this chronic excess demand.

12. Table 9.3 shows the subsidy level and welfare loss implied by the income transfers from the State to the tenant of public housing, that is, areas BCGH and ABC, respectively. The latter is a traditional measure of welfare costs, based on a measure of compensated demand elasticity. This figure is equal to the sum of the price elasticity and the income elasticity times the share of income spent on the good. In example A we assume this compensated elasticity is -1. Example B assumes the elasticity is -0.7.

13. Hegedüs and Tosics (1988) on the breadth of the grey market in Budapest.

14. See Demsetz (1968) for an analysis of the costs of transacting and the way the marketability of a commodity can affect the willingness to supply and demand a good per unit of time. He shows that on stock exchanges, brokers earn the difference between the prices implied by the lower demand and supply per unit of time – that is, the familiar bid-ask spread on financial assets. For the housing market, the costs of exchanging property in well-developed markets, such as the US or the UK, is on the order of 4 percent to 8 percent, inclusive of realtor's fees and appraisal costs. In reforming economies in which the property rights exchanges are ambiguous, legality is often questionable, contract enforcement clauses are doubtful, and the flow of information about similar sales is trivial or non-existent, it is likely that this marketability premium could be substantial as shown by Daniel and Semjen (1987).

10 The Real Sector Dimension: Constraints on Encouraging the Private Sector

1. The figures for the first four years are from *Economic and Social Statistics* (1985) (Lagos: Nigeria).
2. Onibokun (1986).
3. This figure is not unusual for those developing countries that have reasonable regulatory regimes.
4. Uko (1992) discusses the case of the unsubscribed common stock shares for the Nigerian cement producer Nigercem. According to Uko, despite bright industry prospects, investors were wary because of the heavy involvement of government in the company.
5. As far as government transfers are concerned, an issue that also merits consideration is the structure of compensation for employees. As a rule housing allowances are granted in cash or in kind, and equal to 50 percent of basic salary as median for middle management and much higher for senior management. Especially, since allowances may not be reported for personal taxation, it confers a greater purchasing power on these employees and has a significant effect on the price of housing, apart from making the taxation system less transparent and progressive.
6. See Hawkins (1993) for a more detailed analysis of Nigeria's banking system.
7. *Business and Financial Analyst* (1992).
8. *Daily Times* (1992).
9. This and other deficiencies are discussed in greater detail in the *Business and Financial Analyst* (1992).
10. Golembe and Dembitz (1976) offer a thorough analysis of the capital requirements of S&Ls.
11. *The Guardian* (1992).
12. This is the actual 1992 inflation rate for Mexico. In addition, the Ghanian rate is the expected rate for 1992 which in fact was exceeded. By 1995 inflation in Ghana exceeded 50 percent per year, a rate that poses problems for any form of indexation.
13. Federal Republic of Nigeria (1985) contains the recommendations implemented in the 1991 policies. It is worth noting that the inflation rate at the time of these recommendations in 1985 was 5 percent per annum, so that the low interest-rate proposals of the recommendations were much more innocuous than they are now when inflation is much higher.

References

Agbola Tunde and C.O. Olatubara (1989) 'Housing Subsidy, Mortgage Default, and Housing Replicability in Nigeria: A Case Study of the Public Housing Delivery System', *African Urban Quarterly*, vol. 4, nos 1 & 2, Feb. and May, pp. 90–6.

Alexeev, Michael *et al.* (1991) *Overview of the Soviet Housing Sector* (Washington, DC: USAID).

Alexeev, Michael (1988) 'Market vs Rationing: The Case of Soviet Housing', *Review of Economics and Statistics*, vol. LXX, no. 3, Aug.

Alm, James and Robert M. Buckley (1994) 'Privatization by Local Government: A Net Worth Perspective', *Environment and Planning* vol. 12, no. 3, Aug. 1994 pp. 333–346.

Andrusz, Gregory (1990) 'A Note on the Financing of Housing in the Soviet Union', *Soviet Studies*, July.

Bailey, M.J. (1956) 'The Welfare Cost of Inflationary Finance', *Journal of Political Economy*, vol. LXIV, no. 2, April.

Barro, R.J. (1975) 'Monetary Correction, Capital Markets and Open-Market Operations in Colombia', *Journal of Economic Studies*, vol. 2, no. 1, May, pp. 1–9.

Barth, James and R. Dan Brumbaugh (1994) 'Risk Based Capital: Informational and Political Issues', in Charles Stone and Anne Zissn (eds), *Global Risk Based Capital Regulations*, vol. 1 (New York: Irwin).

Berry, R.A. and R. Soligo (1980) *Economic Policy and Income Distribution in Colombia* (Boulcher: Westview Press).

Berry, R.A. and M. Urrutia (1976) *Income Distribution in Colombia* (New Haven: Yale University Press).

Bertaud, Alain and Bertrand Renaud (1995) 'Cities Without Land Markets', in World Bank, *Working Papers*.

Blanchard, Olivier, Rudeger Dornbusch, Paul Krugman, Richard Layard, and Lawrence Summers (1991) *Reform in Eastern Europe* (Cambridge, Mass.: Massachusetts Institute of Technology Press).

Bleaney, M.F. (1988) *Do Socialist Economies Work? The Soviet and East European Experience* (Oxford: Basil Blackwell).

Boléat, Mark (1985) *National Housing Finance Systems: A Comparative Study* (London: Croom Helm in association with the International Union of Building Societies and Savings Associations).

Boschen, John and John Newman (1986) 'Monetary Determinants of the Real Interest Rate in an Open Economy: Evidence from the Argentine Indexed Bond Market', working paper, Department of Economics, the Center for Latin American Studies (New Orleans: Tulane University).

Boskin, Michael (1978) 'Taxation, Saving and the Rate of Interest', *Journal of Political Economy*, special issue, pp. S3–S28.

193

Brownstone, John and Peter Englund (1988) 'Tax Reform and Housing Demand: The Distribution of Welfare Gains and Losses', *European Economic Review*, September.

Buckley, Robert (1991) 'The Measurement, Targeting and Control of Housing Finance Subsidies: The Case of Argentina', *Public Finance*, vol. 46, no. 3, pp. 355–72.

Buckley, Robert (1994) 'Housing Finance in Developing Countries: The Role of Credible Contracts', *Economic Development and Cultural Change*, vol. 42, no. 2, January, pp. 317–32.

Buckley, Robert and John Ermisch (1982) 'Econometric modeling of the effective government policies on house prices', *Oxford Bulletin of Economics and Statistics*, November.

Buckley, Robert and David Gross (1985) 'Selective Credit Policies and the Mortgage Market', *Journal of Money, Credit, and Banking*, vol. 17, no. 3, August, pp. 358–70.

Buckley, Robert and Stephen Mayo (1989) 'Housing Policy in Developing Countries: Evaluating the Macroeconomic Impacts', *Review of Urban and Regional Development*, vol. 1, no. 2, July, pp. 27–48.

Buckley, Robert, James Alm, Edward Kane and Robert Van Order (1989) 'Cushioning Adjustment Costs: The Use of Debt or Subsidies for Housing' Mimeo (Washington, DC: USAID and the World Bank) May.

Buckley, Robert, Barbara Lipman and Thakoor Persaud (1993) 'Mortgage Design Under Inflation and Real Wage Uncertainty: The Use of a Dual Indexed Instrument', *World Development*, vol. 21, no. 3, February, pp. 455–64.

Buckley, Robert, Patric Hendershott and Kevin Villani (1995) 'Rapid Housing Privatization in Reforming Economies: Pay the Special Dividend Now', *Journal of Real Estate Economics and Finance*, vol. 10, no. 1, pp. 63–80.

Bulow, Jeremy and Lawrence Summers (1984) 'The Taxation of Risky Assets' *Journal of Political Economy*, vol. 92, no. 1, pp. 20–42.

Burns, Leland and Leo Grebler (1976) 'Resource Allocation to Housing Investment: A Comparative International Study', *Economic Development and Cultural Change*, October, pp. 95–122.

Business and Financial Analyst (1992) 'National Housing Fund: An Octopus?', Lagos, Nigeria, pp. 8–10.

Byatt, I.C.R., A.E. Holmans and D.E.W. Laidler (1973) 'Income and the Demand for Housing: Some Evidence for Great Britain,' *Economic Notes*, no. 1 (London: Department of the Environment).

Cardoso, Eliana and Rudiger Dornbusch (1987) 'Brazil's Tropical Plan'. papers and proceedings, *American Economic Review*, vol. 77, no. 2, May, pp. 288–92.

Cardoso, Eliana and Albert Fishlow (1989) 'Latin American Economic Development: 1950–80' (Cambridge: National Bureau of Economic Research) November.

Carrizosa, M., C. Fajardo and R. Suescun (1982) *Analisis economico del sistema de valor constante en Colombia* (Centro de Estudios Sobre

Desarrollo Economico, Universidad de los Andes) December.

Castaneda, Tarsicio, and Jorge Quiroz (1986) 'Housing Policies in Chile and Their Redistributive Impact in 1969 and 1980–3', working document (Santiago, Chile: Centro de Estudio Publicos).

Chakravarty, Sukhamoy (Dir. 1985) *Report of the Committee to Review the Working of the Monetary System* (Bombay: Reserve Bank of India).

Chenery, H.B. and M. Syrquin (1975) *Patterns of Development, 1950–70* (Oxford: Oxford University Press).

Compendium of Human Settlements Statistics (1985) (New York: United Nations).

Correa, M.C. (1986) 'Consideraciones sobre el regimen de inversiones por zonas del sistema bancario y el impuesto inflacionario', *Ensayos sobre politica economica*, no. 9, June, pp. 11–42.

Cuddington, J. (1986) 'Bonanzas de productos sasicos, establizacion macroeconomic a y reform a comercial en Colombia', *Ensayos sobre politica economica*, no. 10, December, pp. 45–100.

Cunningham, D.F. and Patric H. Hendershott (1984) 'Pricing FHA Mortgage Default Insurance', *Housing Finance Review*, October, pp. 373–92.

Currie, Lauchlin (1974) 'The "Leading Sector" Model of Growth in Developing Countries', *Journal of Economic Studies*, May.

Currie, Lauchlin (1987) 'The mobilization of savings for housing under conditions of inflation', Mimeo, Bogota, November.

Currie, Lauchlin and F. Rosas (1986) 'UPAC – A Theory Converted into a Successful Reality', *Colombian System of Savings and Housing* (Bogota: Instituto Colombiano de Ahorro y Vivienda).

Dailami, M. (1989) 'Policy Changes that Encourage Private Business Investment in Colombia', *World Bank Staff Working Paper* (Washington, DC: The World Bank) August.

Daily Times (1992) 'FG Releases N250m grant to National Housing Fund', 9 Sep., p. 4, Lagos, Nigeria.

Daniel, Zsuzsa (1984) 'Housing Demand in a Shortage Economy', *Acta Oeronomica*, vol. 41, no. 2, pp. 359–72.

Daniel, Zsuzsa (1985) 'The Effect of Housing Allocation on Social Inequality in Hungary', *Journal of Comparative Economics*, vol. 9, no. 4, December, pp. 391–409.

Daniel, Zsuzsa and Andres Semjen (1987) 'Housing Shortage and Rents: The Hungarian Experience', *Economics of Planning*, vol. 21, no. 1, pp. 13–29.

Davidson, J.E., D.H. Hendry, F. Srba and S. Yeo (1978) 'Econometric Modelling of the Aggregate Time-Series Relationship Between Consumer Expenditure and Income in the United Kingdom', *Economic Journal*, vol. 88, no. 352, pp. 661–92.

De Long, Bradford and Lawrence Summers (1986) 'Is Increased Price Flexibility Stabilizing?', *American Economic Review*, vol. 76, no. 5, December, pp. 1031–44.

Demsetz, Harold (1968) 'The Cost of Transacting', *Quarterly Journal of Economies*, August.

Department of the Environment (1977) *Housing Policy: A Consultative Document* Cmnd 6851 (London: HMSO).

Diaz-Alejandro, Carlos (1970) *Essays on the Economic History of the Argentine Republic* (New Haven, CT: Yale University Press).

Diaz-Alejandro, Carlos (1985) 'Comments on Inflation and Indexation: Argentina' in John Williamson (ed.), *Inflation and Indexation* (Washington, DC: Institute for International Economics).

Diamond, Douglas and Michael Lea (1992) *Housing Finance in Developed Countries: An International Comparison of Efficiency* (Washington, DC: Federal National Mortgage Association).

Dougherty, Ann, and Robert van Order (1982) 'Inflation, Housing Costs and the Consumer Price Index,' *American Economic Review*, vol. 72, no. 1, pp. 154–64.

Easterly, William and Stanley Fischer (1993) 'The Soviet Decline: Historical and Republican Data' (Washington, DC: World Bank).

Economic and Social Statistics (1985) (Lagos, Nigeria: Federal Office of Statistics).

Elias, V.J. (1978) 'Sources of Economic Growth in Latin American Countries', *Review of Economics and Statistics*, vol. LX, no. 3, August, pp. 362–70.

Fabozzi, Frank and Franco Modigliani (1992) *Mortgage and Mortgage-Backed Securities Markets* (Cambridge, Mass.: Harvard Business School Press).

Federal Republic of Nigeria (1985) *The Report of the Special Committee on New National Housing Policy*, July.

Feldstein, Martin (1982) 'Inflation, Tax Rules, and the Accumulation of Residential and Nonresidential Capital', *Scandinavian Journal of Economics*, vol. 31, no. 3, pp. 293–311.

Fischer, S. and Alan Gelb (1990) 'Issues in Socialist Economy Reform', *World Bank Working Paper 565* (Washington, DC: World Bank) December.

Fischer, S. (1975) 'The Demand for Index Bonds', *Journal of Political Economy*, vol. 83, no. 3, June.

Fishlow, Albert (1974) 'Indexing Brazilian Style: Inflation Without Tears?', *Brookings Papers on Economic Activity*, 1 pp. 261–82.

Fons, Jerome (1987) 'The Default Premium and Corporate Bond Experience', *Journal of Finance*, March, pp. 81–98.

Friedman, Benjamin (1985) 'Portfolio Choice and the Debt-to-Income Ratio', *American Economic Review*, vol. 75, no. 2, May, pp. 338–43.

Friedman, Milton (1974a) 'Using Escalators to Help Fight Inflation', *Fortune*, July.

Friedman, Milton (1974b) *Monetary Correction – a Proposal for Escalator Clauses to Reduce the Costs of Ending Inflation* (London: Institute of Economic Affairs).

Fry, M. (1988) *Money, Interest and Banking in Economic Development* (Baltimore: Johns Hopkins University Press).

Furstenberg, George von (1976) 'Distribution Effects of GNMA Home Mortgage Purchases and Commitments under the Tandem Plans', *Journal of Money, Credit, and Banking*, vol. 8, August, pp. 373–89.

Goldsmith, Raymond (1969) *Financial Structure and Development* (New Haven, Conn.: Yale University Press).

Goldsmith, Raymond W. (1985) *Comparative National Balance Sheets: A Study of Twenty Countries, 1688–1978* (Chicago: Chicago University Press).

Golembe, Carter H. and Lewis N. Dembitz (1976) 'Capital Needs of S&L Associations', *Change in the Savings and Loan Industry*, Proceedings of the Second Annual Conference of the Federal Loan Bank of San Francisco, 9–10 Dec.

Gottlieb, Manuel (1976) *Long Swings in Urban Development* (New York: Columbia University Press and National Bureau of Economic Research).

Grimes, Orville (1976) *Housing for Low-Income Urban Families*, World Bank Publication (Baltimore: Johns Hopkins University Press).

The Guardian, 'Problems with Provident Fund', Lagos, March 1992.

Gultekin, Bulent N. (1983) 'Stock Market Returns under Inflation', *Journal of Finance*, March, pp. 49–66.

Hadjimatheou, G. (1976) *Housing and Mortgage Markets: The UK Experience* (London: Saxon House).

Hanson, J.A., F.D. McCarthy and J.A. Kwon (1985) 'Sources of Growth in Colombia, 1963–80', *Journal of Economic Studies*, vol. 12, no. 4, pp. 3–14.

Harberger, Arnold (1969) 'La Tasa de rendimiento de kapital en Colombia', *Revista de la nacion y desarrollo*, vol. 2, no. 1.

Harberger, Arnold (1970) 'Discussion', *Housing and Monetary Policy*, Proceedings of the Monetary Conference (Boston: Federal Reserve Bank of Boston).

Hawkins, Tony (1993) 'A Sector that Needs Reform', *Financial Times*, 1 April, iii: 4. Lagos, Nigeria.

Hayashi Fumio, T. Ito and Joel Slemrod (1988) 'Housing Finance Imperfections: A Comparative Stimulation Analysis of the US and Japan', *Journal of Japanese and International Economics*, vol. 3, pp. 215–38.

Hegedüs, J. and I. Tosics (1988) 'Housing Classes and Housing Policy: Some Changes in the Budapest Housing Market', *International Journal of Urban and Regional Research*, July, pp. 129–36.

Hendershott, Patric H. (1984) 'Development and Equity Returns Revisited', *National Bureau of Economic Research Working Paper*, no. 1521.

Hendershott, Patric H. and Edward J. Kane (1992) 'Causes and Consequences of the 1980s Commercial Construction Boom', *Journal of Applied Corporate Finance*, Spring, pp. 567–82.

Hendershott, Patric and S.C. Hu (1980) 'Government-Induced Bases in the Allocation of the Stock of Fixed Capital in the United States', in George von Furstenberg (ed), *Capital Efficiency and Growth* (Ballinger: Harper & Row).

Hendry, David (1981) 'Economic Modelling of House Prices in the United Kingdom', in D. Hendry and K. Wallis, *Econometrics and Quantitative Economics* (Oxford: Oxford University Press).

Heyman, Daniel (1987) 'The Austral Plan', papers and proceedings, *American Economic Review*, vol. 77, no. 2, May, pp. 280–9.

Hills, John (1991) 'Distributional Effects of Housing Subsidies in the United Kingdom', *Journal of Public Economics*, vol. 44, pp. 321–52.

Ibottson, R. and L. Siegel (1983) 'The World Market Wealth Portfolio', *Journal of Portfolio Management*, Winter, pp. 4–23.

Isaza, F.G. (1987) *El Upac la politica economica y la construccion 1970–87* (Bogota: CAMACOL).

Jorgenson, D.W. and Z. Griliches (1967) 'The Explanation of Productivity Change', *Review of Economic Studies*, vol. xxxiv(3), no. 99, pp. 249–83.

Kalinina, Natalia (1992) 'An Account of Housing Privatization in Russia', *Russian Academy of Sciences Report of the World Bank Technical Cooperation Project* (Washington, DC: World Bank) June.

Katsura, Harold and Raymond Struyk (1992) 'Selling Eastern Europe's Social Housing Stock: Proceed with Caution', *Urban Institute*, January.

Kearl, J. R. (1979) 'Inflation, Mortgages and Housing', *Journal of Political Economy*, no. 87, pp. 1115–38.

Kelley, Allen and Jeffrey Williamson (1984) *What Drives Third World City Growth?* (Princeton: Princeton University Press).

Khan, A.H. and M. Ahmad (1985) 'Real Money Balances in the Production Function of a Developing Country', *Review of Economics and Statistics*, vol. xvii, no. 2, May, pp. 336–40.

Khan, Moshin and Hadeem Ul Hague (1987) 'Capital Flight from Developing Countries', *Finance and Development*, Spring, pp. 23–31.

Kingsley, Tom and Marian Maxiam (1992) 'Housing Costs and Affordability in Czechoslovakia: The Opportunity for Private Home Building', *Urban Institute*, April.

Kingsley, Tom and Raymond Struyk (1992) 'Progress in Privatization: Transforming Eastern Europe's Social Housing', *Urban Institute*, April.

Kontagora, M.T. (1992) 'National and State Housing Policies: An Assessment of On-Going Programmes', speech, 24 March.

Kornai, Janos (1986) 'The Hungarian Reform Process, Visions, Hopes, and Reality', *Journal of Economic Literature*, December, pp. 1687–737.

Kornai, Janos (1990) *The Road to Freedom: Shifting from a Social system the Example of Hungary* (New York: Norton).

Kornai, Janos (1992) *The Socialist System: The Political Economy of Communism* (Princeton, New Jersey: Princeton University Press).

Krueger, Anne (1966) 'Some Economic Costs of Exchange Control: The Turkish Case', *Journal of Political Economy*, October.

Laidler, David (1968) 'The Permanent-Income Concept in a Macro-Economic Model', *Oxford Economic Papers*, vol. 20, no. 1, pp. 11–23.

Laidler, David (1969) 'Income Tax Incentives for Owner-Occupied Housing', in Arnold Harberger and Martin Bailey (eds), *The Taxation of Income from Capital* (Washington, DC: Brookings Institute).

Lessard, D. and Franco Modigliani (1975) 'Inflation and the Housing Market: Problems and Potential Solutions', in Donald Lessard and Franco Modigliani (eds), *New Mortgage Designs for Stable Housing in an Inflationary Environment* (Boston: Federal Reserve Bank of Boston).

Levhari, D. and D. Patinkin (1968) 'The Role of Money in a Simple Growth Model', *American Economic Review*, no. 58, September, pp. 713–54.

Lowery, Ira (1992) 'Real Estate Tenure and Taxation in the Russian Federation', *The Urban Institute*, June.

Mallon, Jorge and Juan Sourrouville (1975) *Economic Policy Making in a Conflict Society* (New Haven, CT: Yale University Press).

Malpezzi, Stephen and Stephen Mayo (1987a) 'The Demand for Housing in Developing Countries: Empirical Estimates from Household Data', *Economic Development and Cultural Change*, December, pp. 687–722.

Malpezzi, Stephen and Stephen Mayo (1987b) 'User Cost and Housing Tenure in Developing Countries', *Journal of Development Economics*, February, pp. 197–220.

Malpezzi, Stephen, Stephen Mayo and David Gross (1985) 'Housing Demand in Developing Countries' *World Bank Staff Working Paper*, no. 733 (Washington, DC: The World Bank).

Matras, Hanna (1989) 'Structure and Performance of the Housing Sector of Centrally Planned Economies', *World Bank, INU Report 53*.

Maydon, Marin, *et al.* (1988) 'El Papel de la Banca de Fomento en el Financiamiento del Sector de la Vivienda' ('The Role of the Banking Sector in the Development of Finance for the Housing Sector') (Lima, Peru: Asociacion Latinamericana de Instituciones Financieras de Desarrollo).

Mayes, D. (1979) *The Property Boom: The Effects of Building Society Behavior on House Prices* (London: Martin Robertson).

Mayo, Stephen (1986) 'Sources of Inefficiency in Subsidized Housing Programs: A Comparison of US and German Experience', *Journal of Urban Economics*, October, pp. 521–36.

Mayo, Stephen and Sholmo Angel (1992) *Housing Indicators Project* (Washington, DC: World Bank).

Mayo, Stephen and James Stein (1995) 'Housing and Labor Market Distortions in Poland', *Housing Economics*, September, pp. 311–24.

McKinnon, Ronald (1991) *The Order of Economic Liberalization Financial Control in the Transition to a Market Economy* (Baltimore: Johns Hopkins University Press).

McKinnon, Ronald (1973) *Money and Capital in Economic Development* (Washington, DC: Brookings Institute).

McNelis, Paul (1988) 'Indexation and Stabilization: Theory and Experience', *World Bank Research Observer*, vol. 3, no. 2, July, pp. 157–69.

Meltzer, Allan (1974) 'Credit Availability and Economic Decisions: some evidence from the mortgage and housing markets', *Journal of Finance*, vol. 29, no. 3, June, pp. 763–77.

Meyer, L.H. (1974) 'Lagged Adjustment in Simple Macro Models', *Oxford Economic Papers*, vol. 26, no. 3, pp. 334–49.

Mills, Edwin S. (1987) 'Has the United States Overinvested in Housing?', *AREUEA Journal*, vol. 15, no. 1, Spring, pp. 601–17.

Minford, Patrick, Michael Peel and Paul Ashton (1987) *The Housing Morass: Regulation, Immobility, and Unemployment*, Hobart Paperback no. 25 (London: Institute of Economic Affairs).

Modigliani, F. (1977) 'The Monetarist Controversy or, Should We Forsake Stabilization Policies?', *American Economic Review*, vol. 67, no. 2, March, pp. 1–19.

Mohan, Rakesh (1987) 'The Strategy for Housing and Urban Development: Some New Perspectives', *Planning Commission*, New Delhi, 1987, mimeographed.

Montenegro, A. and M.A. Garcia (1986) 'Evolucion del Coeficiente Efectivo', *Economia Nacional*, January, pp. 32–9.

Morris, Felipe (1985) 'India's Financial System: An Overview of its Principal Structural Features', *World Bank Staff Working Paper*, no. 739 (Washington, DC: The World Bank).

Muellbauer, John (1992) 'Anglo-German Differences in Housing Market Dynamics: The Role of Institutions and Macro Policy', *European Economic Review*, May, pp. 539–48.

Murie, A.S., P. Niner and C. Watson (1976) *Housing Policy and The Housing System* (London: Allen & Unwin).

Murray, Michael (1983) 'Subsidized and Unsubsidized Housing Starts: 1961–77', *Review of Economics and Statistics*, November, pp. 590–7.

Newberry, David (1992) 'Reform in Hungary: Sequencing and Privatization', in Graham Bird (ed.), *Economic Reform in Eastern Europe* (London: Edward Elgar).

Olsen, Marcur (1982) *The Rise and Decline of Nations* (New Haven, CT: Yale University Press).

Onibokun, Poju (1986) *Urban Housing in Nigeria* (Ibadan, Nigeria: National Institute of Social and Economic Research).

Penner, R.G. and W.L. Silber (1973) 'The Interaction between Federal Credit Programs and the Impact on the Allocation of Credit', *American Economic Review*, vol. 63, no. 5, pp. 838–52.

Poterba, James M. (1992) 'Taxation and Housing: Old Questions, New Answers', *The American Economic Review*, vol. 82, no. 2, May, pp. 237–42.

Prell, Michael (1989) 'The Role of Housing in Soviet GNP Estimates', *Review of Income and Wealth*, vol. 13, no. 3, September, pp. 297–316.

Renaud, Bertrand (1980) 'Resource Allocation to Housing Investment: Comment and Further Results', *Economic Development and Cultural Change*, January.

Renaud, Bertrand (1991) *Housing Reform in Socialist Economies* (World Bank) April.

Renaud, Bertrand (1984) 'Housing and Financial Institutions in Developing Countries: An Overview.' *World Bank Staff Working Paper*, No. 658 (Washington, DC: World Bank).

Reyes, C. (1987) 'Tendencias del empleo y la distribucion del ingreso', *El Problema Laboral Colombia*, October, pp. 389–400.

Romer, P.M. (1987) 'Crazy Explanations for the Productivity Slowdown', *NBER Macroeconomics Annual*, pp. 314–37.

Rosen, Harvey (1979) 'Housing Decisions and the US Income Tax', *Journal of Public Economics*, no. 1, pp. 1–24.

Sandilands, R.J. (1980) *Monetary Correction and Housing Finance in Colombia, Brazil, and Chile* (Aldershot: Gower).

Shah Report, *Finance for Housing Schemes* (1978) (Bombay: Reserve Bank of India).

Short, E.D. (1979) 'A New Look at Real Money Balances as a Variable in the Production Function', *Journal of Money, Credit and Banking*, vol. 11, no. 3, August, pp. 326–39.

Silveira, Ricardo (1989) 'The Evolution of Rent Control in Brazil', *INURD Working Paper*, no. 48 (Washington, DC: World Bank).

Sinai, A. and H.H. Stokes (1972) 'Real Money Balances: An Omitted Variable from the Production Function?' *Review of Economics and Statistics*, no. 54, August, pp. 290–96.

Sinai, A. and H.H. Stokes (1977) 'Real Money Balances as a Variable in the Production Function – A Further Reply by Allen Sinai and Houston Stokes', *Journal of Money Credit and Banking*, vol. 9, May, pp. 372–3.

Sinai, A. and H.H. Stokes (1981) 'Money and the Production Function – A Reply to Boyes and Kavanaugh', *Review of Economics and Statistics*, vol. lxiii, no. 2, May, pp. 313–18.

Solow, R.M. (1957) 'Technical Change and the Aggregrate Production Function', *Review of Economics and Statistics*, vol. 39, no. 3, August, pp. 312–20.

Solow, R.M. (1988) 'Nobel Address', *American Economic Review*, June, pp. 307–17.

Summers, Lawrence (1981) 'Capital Taxation and Accumulation in a Life Cycle Growth Model', *American Economic Review*, September, pp. 533–44.

Sylla, Richard (1991) *A History of Interest Rates* (New Brunswick: Rutgers University Press).

Szelenyi, Ivan and Conrad, J. (1983) *Urban Inequalities Under State Socialism* (New York: Oxford University Press).

Tanzi, Vita (1991) 'Mobilization of Savings in Eastern European Countries: The Role of the State', in Anthony Atkinson and Renato Brunetta, (eds), *Economics for the New Europe* (New York: New York University Press).

Tait, Alan and Peter Heller (1982) 'International Comparisons of Government Expenditures', *International Monetary Fund Occasional Paper 10* (Washington, DC: International Monetary Fund).

Taylor, Lance (1981) *Structuralist Macroeconomics* (New York: Basic Books).

Tideman, Nicholas (1994) 'Public Land Ownership in Reforming Socialist Economies', *Environment and Planning: C*, vol. 12, no. 3, August, pp. 286–97.

Timberg, Thomas and C.V. Aiyar (1984) 'Informal Credit Markets in India', *Economic Development and Cultural Change*, October, pp. 43–60.

Tolley, George S. (1991) 'Urban Housing Reform in China: An Economic Analysis', *World Bank Working Paper 123* (Washington, DC: World Bank) April.

Uko, Inyang Joseph (1992) 'Public Unimpressed by Nigerian Ownership', *The Guardian*, Lagos, 12 April, A11.

Urrutia, M. (1985) *Winners and Losers in Colombia's Economic Growth of the 1970a* (Oxford: Oxford University Press).

US Department of Commerce, Bureau of Economic Analysis (1987) *Fixed Reproducible Tangible Wealth in the United States* (Washington, DC: Government Printing Office).

US Office of Management and Budget, Office of the President (1986) *Special Analysis of the Budget* (Washington, DC).

Veneroso, Frank (1983) 'Chile: Housing finance', Project Brief Appendix, Background Paper for a Housing Finance Project in Chile (Washington, DC: World Bank).

White, Michelle J. and Lawrence J. White (1977) 'The Tax Subsidy to Owner Occupied Housing: Who Benefits', *Journal of Public Economics*, vol. 7, no. 1, February, pp. 111–26.

Whitehead, C.M.E. (1971) 'Inflation and the New Housing Market', *Oxford Bulletin of Economics and Statistics*, vol. 35, no. 4, November, pp. 275–94.

Wilkinson, R.K. (1973) 'The Income Elasticity of the Demand for Housing', *Oxford Economic Papers*, vol. 26, no. 3, pp. 334–49.

Williamson, Oliver E. (1985) *The Economic Institutions of Capitalism* (New York: Free Press).

World Bank (1975) *Housing: Sector Policy Paper* (Washington, DC: World Bank) May.

World Bank (1980) *Shelter, Poverty and Basic Needs* (Washington, DC: World Bank) September.

World Bank (1983a) *Colombia: Economic Development and Policy Under Changing Conditions* (Washington, DC: The World Bank).

World Bank (1983b) *China: Socialist Economic Development 1991* (Washington, DC: World Bank).

World Bank (1985) *Financial Intermediation Policy Paper* (Washington, DC: World Bank).

World Bank (1987) *Colombia: Country Economic Memorandum*, report no. 6626-CO (Washington, DC: The World Bank) October.

World Bank (1989) *World Development Report* (New York: Oxford University Press).

World Bank (1989) *Sustaining the Structural Adjustment Program: A Shelter Strategy for Ghana*, report no. 8099-GH, December.

World Bank (1991a) *China: Urban Housing Reform: Issues and Implementation Options*, report no. 9222-CHA, February.

World Bank (1991b) *Housing Policy Reform in Hungary*, report no. 9031-HU, May.

World Bank (1991c) *Staff Appraisal Report for the Republic of Poland: First Housing Project*, report no. 9853-POL, September.

World Bank (1992b) *Russian Economic Reform: Crossing the Threshold of Structural Change*, Country Study, September, pp. 222–34.

World Bank (1992c) *World Development Report*, various years: Development and the Environment (New York: Oxford University Press).

World Bank (1993) 'Housing: Enabling Markets to Work', A World Bank Policy Paper (Washington, DC: World Bank).

Yujnovsky, Oscar (1984) *Claves Politica Del Problema Habitacional Argentino 1955–81* (Buenos Aires: Grupo Editor Latinamericano).

Index